OXFORD

geog.1

NEW edition

geography for key stage 3

< rosemarie gallagher > < richard parish > < janet williamson >

OXFORD
UNIVERSITY PRESS

Great Clarendon Street, Oxford OX2 6DP

Oxford University Press is a department of the University of Oxford.
It furthers the University's objective of excellence in research,
scholarship, and education by publishing worldwide in

Oxford   New York

Auckland   Cape Town   Dar es Salaam   Hong Kong   Karachi
Kuala Lumpur   Madrid   Melbourne   Mexico City   Nairobi
New Delhi   Shanghai   Taipei   Toronto

With offices in

Argentina   Austria   Brazil   Chile   Czech Republic   France   Greece
Guatemala   Hungary   Italy   Japan   Poland   Portugal   Singapore
South Korea   Switzerland   Thailand   Turkey   Ukraine   Vietnam

Oxford is a registered trade mark of Oxford University Press
in the UK and in certain other countries

© RoseMarie Gallagher, Richard Parish, Janet Williamson 2005
The moral rights of the author have been asserted
Database right Oxford University Press (maker)

First published 2000

Second Edition 2005

British Library Cataloguing in Publication Data

Data available

ISBN-13: 978 0 19 913449 6
ISBN-10: 0 19 913449 9

10 9 8 7 6 5 4

Acknowledgements

The publisher and authors would like to thank the following for permission to use
photographs and other copyright material:

P4 PLI/Science Photo Library; p7l&r Popperfoto; p8 tr ESA; p8bl&r Oxford University Press; p8 tl& cl PLI/Science Photo Library; p8cr W. Cross/Skyscan; p10 Oxford University Press; p11 Viviane Moos/Corbis UK Ltd.; p12 Oxford University Press; p13 Education Photos; p14 NRSC/Skyscan; p15 Education Photos; p17t Education Photos, p17b Mark Azavedo; p20 Sealand Aerial Photography; p21 Oxford University Press; p24 Oxford University Press; p26 Jason Hawkes/Corbis UK Ltd.; p29bl Ric Ergenbright/Corbis UK Ltd., p29tc C. Moore/Corbis UK Ltd., p29bc Nik Wheeler/Corbis UK Ltd., p29br Charles & Josette Lenars/Corbis UK Ltd., p29t Christophe Loviny/Corbis UK Ltd.; p30 West Stow Anglo-Saxon Village Trust/St Edmundsbury Borough Council; p31 Simmons Aerofilms; p33 Art Directors & Trip Photo Library; p36bcr&cr Alex Hibbs/Oxford University Press; p36bl&br&bcl Martin Sookias/Oxford University Press, p36t Oxford Science Park; p37l Mark Azavedo, p37tr Education Photos; p37br Martin Sookias/Oxford University Press p38bl Leslie Garland Picture Library, p38t Art Directors & Trip Photo Library; p40bl English Partnerships, p40br Glenn Harvey/Rex Features, p40t&c Woodlands Library, Greenwich; p41t&c Chris Henderson/English Partnerships, p41b English Partnerships; p42bl Chris Henderson/English Partnerships, p42br Sam Tinson/Rex Features, p42t English Partnerships; p43tl J. Allan Cash Photo Library, p43bl Oxford University Press, p43tr Telegraph Colour Library/Getty Images, p43br English Partnerships; p44tl&bl Milton Keynes City Discovery Centre, p44tr&br Martin Bond/Photofusion Picture Library; p46t Mary Evans Picture Library; p46b Miichael Taylor/Oxford University Press; p48tl Martin Sookias/Oxford University Press, p48br Michaael Taylor/Oxford University Press; p48r John Powell Photographer/Alamy; p50bl Bluewater, Kent; p50br Tony Kyriacou/Rex Features, p50t Andy Drysdale/Rex Features; p51 Bluewater, Kent; p52 Michael Keller/Corbis UK Ltd.; p53 Alex Segre/Rex Features; p54 Oxford University Press; p56cl WildCountry/Corbis UK Ltd., p56bl David Wrench/LGPL/Alamy, p56cr&br Adam Woolfitt/Corbis UK Ltd., p56t Jason Hawkes/Corbis UK Ltd., p56c Oxford University Press; p57l J. Allan Cash Photo Library,

p57r Barnaby/Mary Evans Picture Library; p59 Oxford University Press; p63cl&bl&cr&t Barnaby's/Mary Evans Picture Library, p63br Hulton|Archive/Getty Images; p65l J. Allan Cash Photo Library, p65r London Aerial Photo Library/Corbis UK Ltd.; p66 Colin McPherson/Sygma/Corbis UK Ltd.; p68tl Bettmann/Corbis UK Ltd., p68cl&cr Tony O'Keefe/Oxford University Press, p68bl&bcl Oxford University Press, p68tr Corel/Oxford University Press, p68b Eddie Ryle-Hodges/Edifice/Corbis UK Ltd., p68bcr Adam Woolfitt/Corbis UK Ltd.; p69l Chris Bland/Eye Ubiquitous/Corbis UK Ltd., p69r Stan Gamester/Photofusion Picture Library/Alamy; p70 Art Underground/Corbis Uk Ltd.; p72 RoseMarie Gallagher; p75 Airfotos/Skyscan; p76t Art Directors & Trip Photo Library, p76b Val Corbett; p78 Art Directors & Trip Photo Library; p77 RoseMarie Gallagher; p79 Landform Slides; p80t ICCE Photolibrary, p80b Corel/Oxford University Press; p81 Heather Angel/Natural Visions; p82 Shropshire Star; p86 Shropshire Star; p87 both; Shropshire Star p88l Abir Abdullah/Still Pictures, p88r Rafiqur Rahman/Reuters/Corbis UK Ltd.; p90tc Reading/Environment Agency, p90tr Martin Sookias/Oxford University Press, p90br Oxford and County Newspapers; p90bl&m Shropshire Star; p91tl&tr&br Panos Pictures; p91bl&tc&bc Popperfoto; p96l Popperfoto/Alamy; p93 Shropshire Star; p94 Tom Purslow/Manchester United/Getty Images; p96r Adam Davy/Empics; p100bl Barry Coombs/Empics, p100cl RoseMarie Gallagher; p100tc&tr&br © Liverpool Football Club; p101 © Liverpool Football Club; p103 Skyscan; p104l&c Barry Coombs/Empics, p104r Ed Kashi/Network Photographers Ltd; p105 Popperfoto; p106 Bernhard Edmaier/Science Photo Library; p108l Corel/Oxford University Press, p108r KTB - Archive of the GeoForschungZentrum Potsdam; p110 Paul A Souders/Corbis UK Ltd.; p113 (Source: World Ocean Floor map by Bruce C. Heezen and Marie Tharp, 1977. Copyright © 1977 Marie Tharp. Reproduced by permission of Marie Tharp, 1 Washington Ave., South Nyack, NY10960)/Marie Tharp; p115 AP Photo; p116l Shehzad Noorani/Still Pictures, p116tr Wolfgang Rattav/Reuters/Corbis UK Ltd., p116br Caren Firouz/Reuters/Corbis UK Ltd.; p118l J. Allan Cash Photo Library, p118r Lyn Topinka/United States Department of the Interior/U.S. Geological Survey; p119t Rex Features; p119b Katz Pictures; p120l Marco Fulle/Osservatorio Astronomico/Trieste; p120r NASA; p121 Kevin West/Liaison Agency/Getty Images; p122tl Yannis Kontos/Sygma/Corbis UK Ltd., p122cl Patrick Robert/Sygma/Corbis UK Ltd., p122bl Alan Andrews Photography/Alamy, p122tc Peter Turnley/Corbis UK Ltd., p122bc Thomas J. Casadevall/United States Department of the Interior/U.S. Geological Survey, p122tr Peter Frischmuth/Still Pictures, p122cr Bryan F. Peterson/Corbis UK Ltd., p122br Popperfoto; p122c Jacques Langevin/Sygma/Corbis UK Ltd.; p123 Sipa Press/Rex Features; p124l A. Tovy/Art Directors & Trip Photo Library, p124r Geoscience Features Picture Library; p125 Corel/Oxford University Press.

The Ordnance Survey map extracts on pp. 23, 24, 32, 35, 38, 39, 86, 103, and 126 are reproduced with the permission of the Controller of Her Majesty's Stationery Office © Crown Copyright.

Illustrations are by James Alexander, Martin Aston, Barking Dog Art, Jeff Bowles, Matt Buckley, Stefan Chabluk, Michael Eaton, Hardlines, Jill Hunt, David Mostyn, Olive Pearson, Colin Salmon, Martin Sanders and Jamie Sneddon.

The publisher and authors would like to thank the many people and organizations who have helped them with their research. In particular: The Environment Agency (and especially the staff at the Shrewsbury office); English Partnerships at the Greenwich Peninsula development; Jonny Popper at London Communications Agency; Chris Talbot at GeoBusiness Solutions Ltd, Wendover; Save the Children; Professor John Bale; Andy Ward; Rogan Taylor; Liverpool Football Club; Chris Fitch of Darlington Borough Council; the staff of the local studies centre at Aylesbury library; Ray Kershaw; Sutton Kersh Estate Agents of Liverpool; and finally Alex 'Walter' Middleton.

We would like to thank our excellent reviewers, who have provided thoughtful and constructive criticism at various stages: Phyl Gallagher, John Edwards, Anna King, Katherine James, Paul Apicella, David Weeks, Richard Farmer, Roger Fetherston, Philip Amor, Louise Ellis, Kathy Fairchild, Janet Wood, Andy Lancaster, David Jones, Bob Drew, Paul Bennett, John Hughes, and Michael Gallagher.

Thanks also to Ann Hayes, Pauline Jones and Omar Farooque for their invaluable help and support.

Cover photo: Getty Images and Hemera.

Printed in Singapore by KHL Printing Co Pte Ltd

Contents

The big picture

Welcome to *geog.1*, the first book of the *geog.123* course.

This course is all about planet Earth, and how and where we live on it. These are the big ideas behind the course:

♦ Humans like us have been here for a very short time, compared to the Earth. (For about 200 000 years, compared with 4.6 billion !)

♦ We have spread over most of the Earth, farming it, mining it, building on it, and carving it up into over 200 countries.

♦ We have changed the Earth as we spread – and spoiled many places.

♦ Now we are learning that we must look after it properly.

♦ The Earth still holds many dangers for us, such as floods and earthquakes. We try to protect ourselves from them.

Your goals for this course

By the end of this course, we hope you'll be a good geographer ! And that means you will:

♦ be interested in the world around you.

♦ understand that many processes, both natural and human, are shaping and changing the Earth.

♦ know what kinds of questions to ask, to find out about countries and places and people.

♦ be able to carry out enquiries, to find answers to your questions.

♦ have the other key skills (such as map reading) that a geographer needs. Your teacher will tell you which ones.

♦ think geography is brilliant !

Did you know ?
♦ The Earth has been here about 23 000 times longer than humans.

Did you know ?
♦ Dinosaurs were around for about 165 million years.
♦ That's over 800 times longer than humans !

Did you know ?
Most experts think that:
♦ humans like us first appeared in East Africa ...
♦ ... and spread out from there.

Your chapter starter

Page 4 shows a planet. Which one ?

Where in space is it ?

What's keeping it there ?

Who's on it ?

What are they doing ?

It's the third one from the sun.

What's geography about?

In this unit you will find out what kinds of things you'll study in geography – and how being nosy will help!

Physical geography
– what planet Earth is like

hazards we face, such as …

… mountains

… volcanic eruptions

… earthquakes

how the Earth is changing

… rivers

natural features, like …

… waterfalls

… rocks

… floods

… …..……
weather and climate

… beaches

… the sea

Human geography
– how and where we live

what life is like in different countries

the places we live in

how rich or poor we are

how and where we shop

HOSPITAL

how and why places grow

what kind of work we do

how the human race is growing

Environmental geography
– how we affect our surroundings

why global warming may be our fault

how we pollute the air …

how we can waste less

how we destroy plants and animals

… and water

BOTTLES

how we spoil places

how we can look after the environment

Be a good geographer

Geography is about the world around you. And the first step to being good at it is: get nosy!

So, use your eyes. Look for clues. Ask questions that start with *Who, What, Where, How, Why, When* …

How is it changing?

Where is this place?

?

Who is affected by the changes?

What is it like?

How do they feel about it?

Why is it like this?

How do *I* feel about it?

Your turn

1 Copy and complete in your own words:
Physical geography is about …
Human geography is about …
Environmental geography is about …

2 Which kind of geography is this topic?
  a how clouds form   b looking for work
  c protecting pandas d where trainers are made
  e caves   f acid rain

3 Photo A below shows people on holiday.
  a Why do you think they chose this place? List as many reasons as you can.
  b After each reason, write *(P)* if it's about physical geography, *(H)* if human, or *(E)* if environmental.

4 Time to get nosy! Study photo B for clues. Then answer these questions:
  a What is going on in the photo?
  b How did the place get to be like this?
  c Who do you think is responsible?

5 a Now make up three new questions about photo B, and what's going on there. No silly ones! (Hint: *Who? What? Where? How? Why? When?*)
  b Ask your partner to try to answer them.

6 Compare the two photos.
  a Can you see any similarities?
  b Do you think there is any connection at all between the two scenes?

A

B

Making and mapping connections

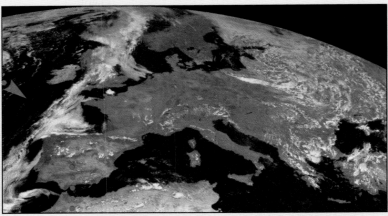

Where is Walter?

On planet Earth, with over 6.4 billion other humans (that's 6 400 000 000) including you …

… in Europe, along with 730 million other humans (that's 730 000 000) …

Everton FC

Liverpool FC

… in the British Isles, with 63 million other humans …

… in Liverpool, with 440 000 other humans …

… in number 181 Anfield Road, with 4 other humans …

… in this room, all alone.

The big picture

This chapter is all about maps, and how to use them. These are the big ideas behind the chapter:

◆ We humans are spread out all over the Earth – but we are still connected to each other in many different ways.

◆ We use maps to show where we live on the Earth, and what places are like.

◆ There are many different kinds of maps.

◆ Using maps is a key skill for a good geographer. (That's you!)

Your goals for this chapter

By the end of this chapter you should be able to answer these questions:

◆ In what ways am I connected to people and places all over the world?

◆ What does the scale on a map or plan tell me?

◆ What are map grid references, and how do I use them to find places?

◆ How can I measure distance on a map?

◆ What are compass points, and how can I use them to give, and follow, directions?

◆ What's the difference between a sketch map and other types of map?

◆ What are OS maps, and what kinds of things are shown on them?

◆ How is the height of the land shown on an OS map? (Two ways!)

And then ...

When you finish the chapter, come back to this page and see if you have met your goals!

Did you know?

◆ 5000 years ago we thought the Earth was flat – and you could fall off.

Did you know?

◆ The world's oldest known maps were found in Iraq.
◆ They are drawn on clay tablets, over 4500 years old.

Did you know?

◆ Today map makers use photos from satellites and planes, to help them map the world.
◆ 200 years ago, they used the position of the sun and stars.

Your chapter starter

You are flying back to planet Earth to find Walter.

You have his address – but you don't want to ask for directions.

Would the images on page 8 help you to find him? Give your reasons.

There are special diagrams that would help you much more. Geographers just adore them. They're called ......?

Where have you been?

Making connections

In this unit you'll see how we are connected to people and places all over the world – and how this can be shown using maps.

Walter connected

Walter. Alone in his room in Liverpool – but connected to people and places everywhere.

Liverpool

His other cousin Kim, who lives in Surrey.

A postcard from Warkworth in Northumberland, where his cousin Violet lives.

In this little white box – a tooth that fell out when he was 8, on a visit to his uncle in Cornwall. (The tooth fairy failed to turn up.)

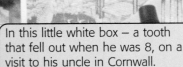

His shades. Made from oil that once lay under the ground in Nigeria.

He gets e-mails every week from his penfriends in Hong Kong and Kenya.

A CD of music he downloaded from a website in Los Angeles. The 'silver' on the CD is aluminium from Jamaica.

This top was sewn last month in China by a lady called Lily. He bought it in Kirkdale, just down the road.

His favourite football team – Liverpool. He's lucky. He lives in Anfield, close to their stadium.

A kite he got last summer in Redwood Village, a holiday camp on the Isle of Man.

His favourite book. A present from his granny who lives in Shrewsbury.

His ancient Walkman – invented in Japan.

Mapping connections

Great Britain

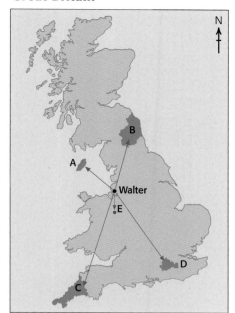

The world

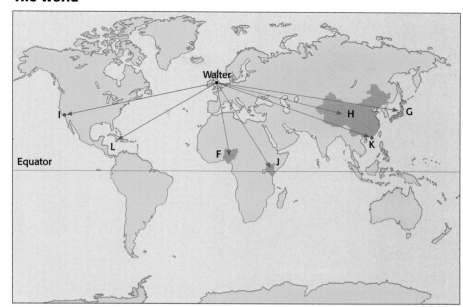

Page 8 showed images of the world, and Europe, and the island where Walter lives (Great Britain). Above are maps of these places.

With maps it is easier to see where places are, and to show connections between them.

The maps above show Walter's connections from page 10 – but that is just the start! All day long he is connected to *hundreds* of people and places – through school, TV, the internet, the things he owns, and the food he eats.

It's just the same for you.

▶ *Lily in China, who sewed Walter's top.*

Your turn

1 Match each letter on the maps above to a place named on page 10. Start like this: A =
(No peeking at the maps at the back of this book!)
Then give your answers to a partner to check.

2 Walter is connected to Jamaica by his CDs. That's an *international* connection. Pick out:
 a two other international connections for him
 b two local connections
 c two national connections
(Try the glossary?)

3 You too are connected to hundreds of places.
 a Make a big table like the one started on the right.
 b Leave room for three places, for each connection. Add more types of connection. (Music, TV, clothes?)
 c Now fill in the table, for yourself.

4 Imagine the UK is cut off from the rest of the world. You can't get news, or post, or TV, or phone calls, or food, or other goods, from outside the UK.
 a List all the things you would have to do without.
 b What three things would you miss most?

Places I am connected to

Place	Connection
London … …	I've been there
… … …	Friends/relatives live there
… …	I eat food that was grown there

Plans and scales

In this unit you will learn what a plan is, and what the scale of the plan tells you.

A photo

This is Walter's room.
He tidied it for the photo.

A plan

This is a **plan** of Walter's room –
a drawing of what you would see
looking down from the ceiling.

A plan is really a map of a small
area – for example a room, or a
house, or your school.

The scale

1 cm on the plan represents 30 cm
in the room. That is the **scale** of
the plan. You can show it in three
ways:

1 In words: **1 cm to 30 cm**

2 As a ratio: **1 : 30**
(say it as *1 to 30*)

3 As a line divided into
centimetres:

0   30   60   90   120 cm

The scale is marked on a plan so
that people can tell the size in
real life.

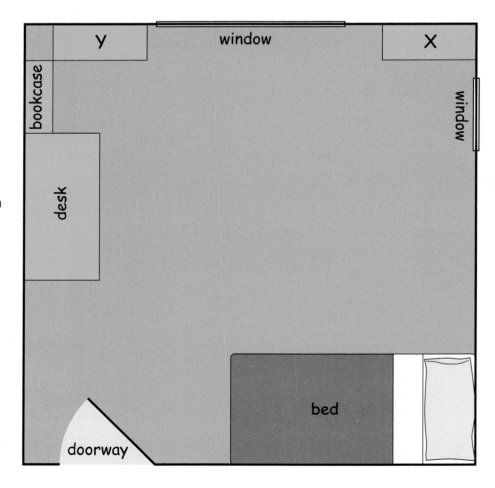

Working out scale

This is the plan of a table in Walter's kitchen. The table is 8 cm long in the plan. It is 160 cm long in real life.

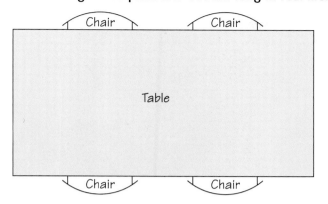

◆ 8 cm on the plan represents 160 cm in real life.

◆ So 1 cm on the plan represents 20 cm in real life.

◆ So you can write the scale as:

   1:20   or   1 cm to 20 cm   or   0   20   40 cm

Be careful with units!

Look at this scale.

0   2   4   6   8   10   12 m

Here 1 cm represents 2 metres.
You can write this as **1:200**.

The 2 metres has been changed to centimetres. That's because *you must use the same units on each side of the* :

1:200 means **1 cm to 200 cm** or **1 cm to 2 m.**

Your turn

1 Look at the plan of Walter's room. What do X and Y represent?

2 On a plan, one wall of a room is shown like this:

  ─────────────────

  The scale of the plan is 1 cm to 60 cm.
  How long is the wall in real life?

3 Below are walls from another plan. This time the scale is 1 : 50. How long is each wall in real life?

  a ──────────────────────

  b ──────────

4 Using a scale of 1 cm to 20 cm, draw a line to represent:
  a 40 cm   **b** 80 cm   **c** 2 metres
  Write the scale beside your lines.

5 If the scale is 1 : 300, what length does each line represent? Give your answer in metres.

  a ──────────

  b ─────────────────────

  c ──────────────

6 Draw a line to represent 1 kilometre, using each of these scales in turn:
  1 cm to 1 km   1 cm to 50 m   1 cm to 100 m
  Write the scale beside your line, in any of the three forms you wish.

7 Make a chart like this and fill it in for Walter's room.

Walter's room	On the plan	In real life
How wide is it? Measure the wall by the desk.		
How long?		
How long is the bed?		
How wide is the big window?		
How wide is the doorway?		

8 Walter is getting a new chest of drawers for his room:

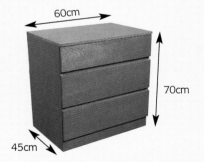

  a To draw a plan of it, which surface will you use?
   the top   the side   the front
  b Draw the plan, to the same scale as Walter's room.
  c Will the chest of drawers fit through the doorway?
  d Where in the room would you put it?

9 Compare the photo and plan of Walter's room.
  a Give three things in the photo that are not on the plan, and suggest reasons why they are not.
  b Is there anything else you'd show on the plan?

Maps and grid references

In this unit you will learn how to find places on a map, using grid references.

An aerial photo

This is an **aerial photo** – a photo taken from the air.

It shows part of the River Mole valley in Surrey. In the top right is the village of Mickleham.

Walter went fishing here when he visited his cousin Kim. (The fish fled.)

> ### Did you know?
> ◆ The first ever aerial photo was taken in France, in 1758 – from a balloon!

A map

This is a **map** of the same place. Compare it with the photo.

Note that the map has:

◆ a title
◆ a frame around it
◆ an arrow to show north
◆ a scale
◆ a key.

A good map should have all five of these things.

Key

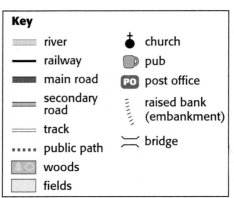

river	✚ church
railway	pub
main road	PO post office
secondary road	raised bank (embankment)
track	bridge
public path	
woods	
fields	

The River Mole valley near Mickleham

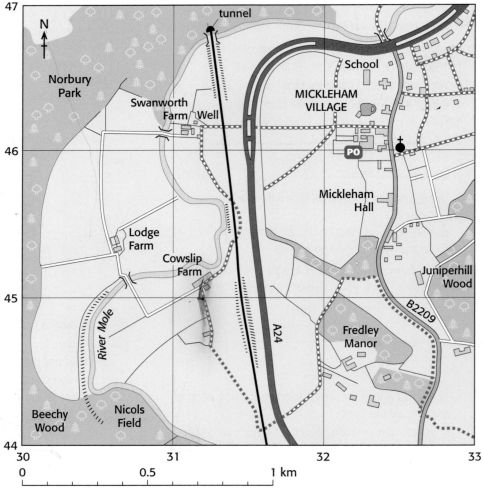

Using grid lines

The map on page 14 has **grid lines** with numbers on. These help you find a place quickly. To find the school in the square with **grid reference** 3246:

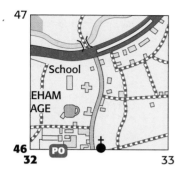

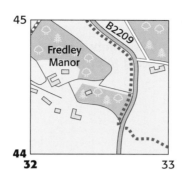

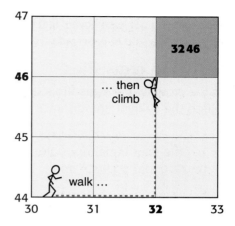

Find the square where lines 32 and 46 meet in the bottom left corner. (It's shown above.) Then look for the school.

In the same way Fredley Manor is in the square with grid reference 3244. Lines 32 and 44 meet in the bottom left corner.

A grid reference gives the number along the bottom first. This shows how to find square 3246. *Walk before you climb!*

These grid references are called **four-figure**. Why?

Six-figure grid references

There is a school *and* a church in square 3246 above.

You can say exactly where each is in the square using a six-figure number. This is what to do:

◆ Divide the sides of the square into ten parts, in your mind, as shown on the right.

◆ Count how many parts you must walk along before you reach the building, and how many parts you must climb.

For the school you go 3 parts along and 5 parts up. So its **six-figure grid reference** is 323465. The one for the church is 325460. Do you agree?

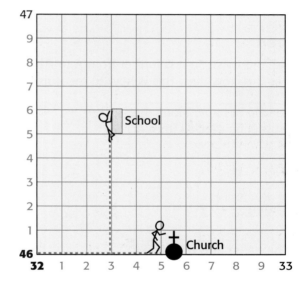

Your turn

1 Look back at the map on page 14. Give a four-figure grid reference for:
   a Mickleham Hall   b Cowslip Farm   c Nicols Field

2 What is at this grid reference on the map?
   a 312468   b 308448   c 309461

3 Give a six-figure grid reference for:
   a Mickleham Hall
   b the post office
   c the pub

4 There is something at 312463 that you can't see on the photo. What is it?

5 You can't see the river on the photo. How can you tell where it is?

6 Describe what you will see, if you stand at 313453 facing south. (With your back to the north!)

7 How far is it from Lodge Farm to Cowslip Farm, along the track? (Think of a way to measure it using the scale.)

8 This shows a signpost in the area. Where do you think it belongs on the map? Write a six-figure grid reference.

9 Now compare the map on page 14 with the plan on page 12. What do you think the differences are, between a map and a plan?

How far?

In this unit you will learn how to find the distance between two places on a map.
You will need a strip of paper with a straight edge.

◼ As the crow flies

'As the crow flies' means the straight line distance between two places.
To find the straight line distance from A to F, this is what to do:

Key
—— road

| **1** Lay the strip of paper on the map, to join points A and F. |

| **2** Mark it at A and F. |

| **3** Now lay the paper along the scale line to find the distance AF. |

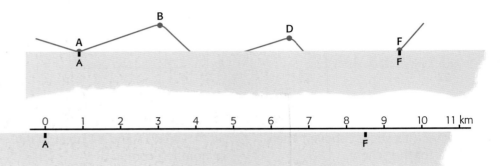

From A to F as the crow flies is 8.5 km

◼ By road

Roads bend and twist. So it is further from A to F by road than as the crow flies. This is how to measure it:

| **1** Lay the strip of paper along the straight section of road from A to B. |

| **2** Mark it at A and B. |

| **3** Pivot the paper at B until it lies along the next straight section, B to C. Mark it at C. |

| **4** Now pivot it at C so that it lies along the next straight section, C to D. Mark it at D. |

| **5** Move along the road in this way, section by section, until you reach F. |

| **6** Place the paper along the scale line to find the distance AF. |

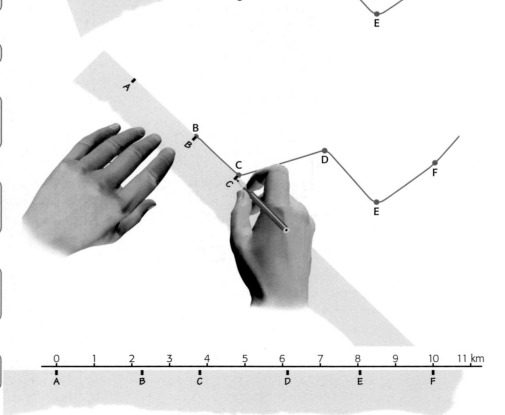

From A to F by road is 10 km

Your turn

The photo and map on page 14 showed part of the River Mole valley in Surrey. This map shows more of the same area. (What do you notice about the scale?)

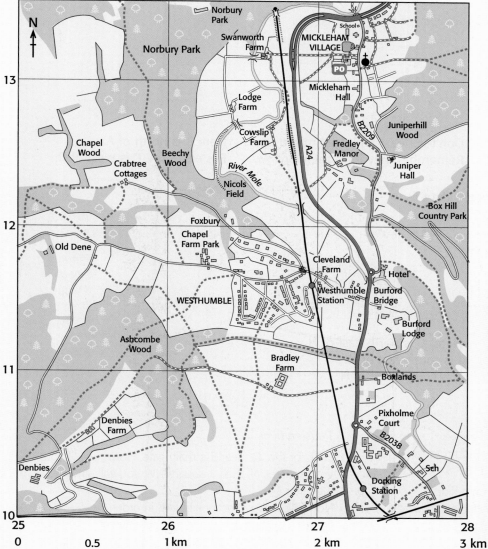

Key

river	woods
railway	fields
main road	
secondary road	
minor road	
track	
public path	
church	
pub	
post office	
raised bank (embankment)	
bridge	
railway station	

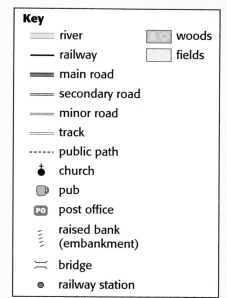

▲ Boxlands.

▲ Juniper Hall.

1 How far is it as the crow flies from Mickleham church to Westhumble station?

2 How far is it by rail from Westhumble station to Dorking station?

3 About how far is it by road from Mickleham Hall (273129) to the hotel at 274117?

4 Walter hired a bike at Westhumble station. He followed these directions:
Go along the short road from the station to the T-junction at Cleveland Farm. Turn left. At the next fork, take the road to the left and cycle for 0.7 km.
Where did he end up?

5 Every day, Kim's mother collects her from school at 276103 and drives her home by this route:
From the school, go right on the B2038.
At the roundabout, take the A24 north for 0.9 km.
Turn left onto the minor road and continue for 0.5 km.
Now take the road to the right and continue for 1.4 km.
Where does Kim live?

6 Juniper Hall and Boxlands are shown above.
  a Find them on the map, and give six-figure grid references for them.
  b Write instructions telling a friend how to get from Juniper Hall to Boxlands. Don't forget distances!

Which direction?

In this unit you will learn how to give and follow directions, using N, S, E and W.

The compass points

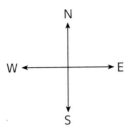

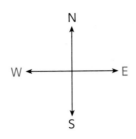

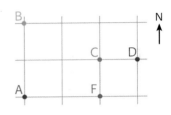

N, S, E, W are the four compass points: north, south, east, west.

Don't get east and west mixed up. Remember they form the word **we**.

Here B is north of A. F is east of A. C is west of D.

We can add other directions in between, like this:

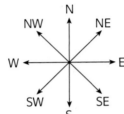

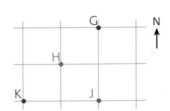

NE stands for north east (or north *of* east). SW stands for south west (or south *of* west).

Here, G is north east of H. J is south east of H. K is south west of H.

Did you know?

- You can use a compass to tell you where N is.
- The compass was invented in China.
- The first one was an iron needle floating in a bowl of water.

Your turn

1 You are standing at C in the first grid above.
  Which direction do you face when you turn towards:
  a F? b D? c A? d B?

2 Page 19 shows where Walter went on holiday.
  The bowling alley is in square D5. What is in square:
  a A10? b F6? c C4? d F2?

3 You are at the hostel. In which direction is :
  a bike hire?
  b the riding school?

4 In which direction would you go, to get to:
  a the duck pond, from the pizza place?
  b the gym, from the bowling alley?
  c bike hire, from the kite shop?

5 How far is it by footpath from the door of the hostel to the door of the bike hire shop?
  You can use your ruler as a linear scale.

6 To get from the cafe to where Walter stayed:
  ◆ From the cafe door, walk 50 m SE, then 65 m N.
  ◆ Next walk 40 m E, then 10 m SE, then 10 m SW.
  Where did he stay?

Treasure hunt

7 Look for the ● near the main gate. From here, if you go 2 squares N, then 1 square NW, you will arrive at the letter **a**.
  Now follow the directions below, in order.
  For each, write down the letter you arrive at.
  The letters will make a word.

  ◆ Start at ●. Go 2 squares W.
  ◆ Then go 8 squares N and 4 squares E.
  ◆ Then go 1 square N and 5 squares W.
  ◆ Next, go 2 squares SE then 4 squares S.
  ◆ Then go 2 squares SW and 1 square SE.
  ◆ Then 3 squares NW, followed by 4 squares E, then 3 squares NE, then 2 squares N.

  What word have you made?

8 a Now choose your own word, with at least 5 letters but not more than 8.
  b Write instructions for making this word, like those in question 7. Start from the ●.
  c Ask a partner to follow the instructions.

Map of your holiday village

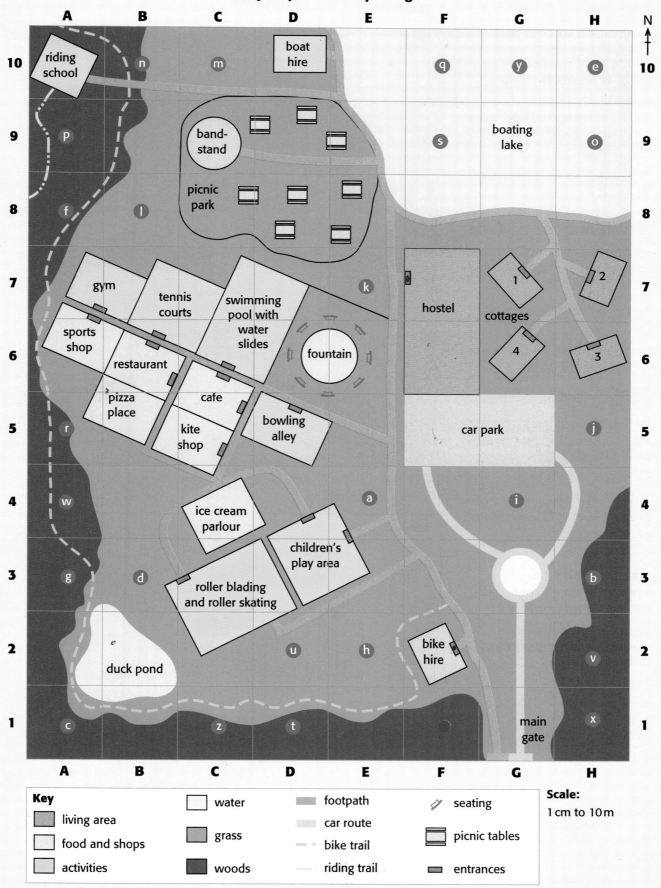

Key

- living area
- food and shops
- activities
- water
- grass
- woods
- footpath
- car route
- bike trail
- riding trail
- seating
- picnic tables
- entrances

Scale:
1 cm to 10 m

Drawing a sketch map

In this unit you'll learn about simple maps you can draw for yourself – sketch maps.

What's a sketch map?

A sketch map is a simple map to do a job – for example to show what a place is like, or how to get from one place to another.

A sketch map can be quite rough. If it does what you want, it's fine !

A sketch map of a place

This photo shows part of Warkworth in Northumberland, where Walter's cousin Violet lives.

Facing you is the remains of a Norman castle.

And below is a sketch map of the same place, which Walter started.

(You have to do one later.)

A sketch map should have:

◆ a title, frame, and key

◆ an N arrow

◆ labels, and annotations (notes), where these help

◆ simple lines

◆ just enough detail to give a rough idea. (Don't show each building, or tree, or rock.)

Sketch maps are not to scale. You can add a note to say this.

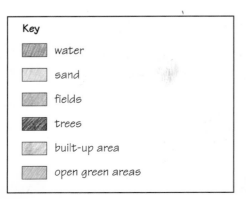

Key
- water
- sand
- fields
- trees
- built-up area
- open green areas

beach sea field river

▲ *Warkworth, from the air.*

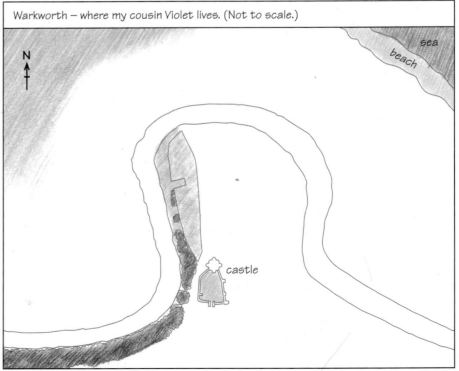

Warkworth – where my cousin Violet lives. (Not to scale.)

N

sea
beach

castle

A sketch map to show a route

This street map shows part of the area around Walter's home in Liverpool. The streets are drawn to scale.

▲ *Walter heads for the post office with a surprise for Violet.*

This sketch map shows Walter's route from his home to the post office. It is not to scale. It has just enough detail to be helpful.

Did you know?
◆ The early explorers made sketch maps of new places they found.
◆ Many took artists along to do drawings.

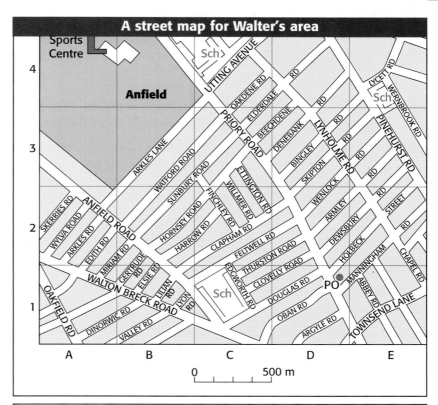
A street map for Walter's area

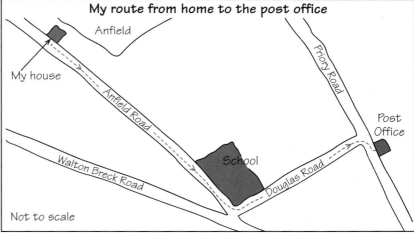
My route from home to the post office

Your turn

1 Draw a sketch map (like the one Walter started) for the photo on page 20. Don't forget a key!

2 Compare the street map and sketch map above.
   a Write down three differences between them.
   b Why was the school marked on the sketch map?

3 Look again at the street map. Walter's house is on Anfield Road, in square A3.
   a Work out an easy route from his house to the school in Wernbrook Road (E4).
   b Now draw a sketch map of the route. Show just enough detail to be helpful.

4 This is Walter's route to his friend Alan's house.
   ◆ Go out my front door, turn left.
   ◆ Take the seventh street on the left, then first right, then first left.
   ◆ Next take the first right, then second left.
   ◆ Alan lives in the second house from the end, on the right hand side of the road.
   a In which street does Alan live?
   b In which direction is it from Walter's house?
   c About how far is it from his house?
   d Draw a sketch map to show his route.

Ordnance Survey maps

In this unit you'll learn what OS maps are, and what they show, and how to use them.

What are OS maps?

Ordnance Survey maps or **OS maps** are maps of places. They are to scale, and give lots of detail. They use symbols to show things.

The OS map opposite shows Warkworth (from page 20), and Amble. The key below has the symbols. (And there's a larger key on page 126.)

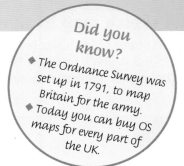

Did you know?
- The Ordnance Survey was set up in 1791, to map Britain for the army.
- Today you can buy OS maps for every part of the UK.

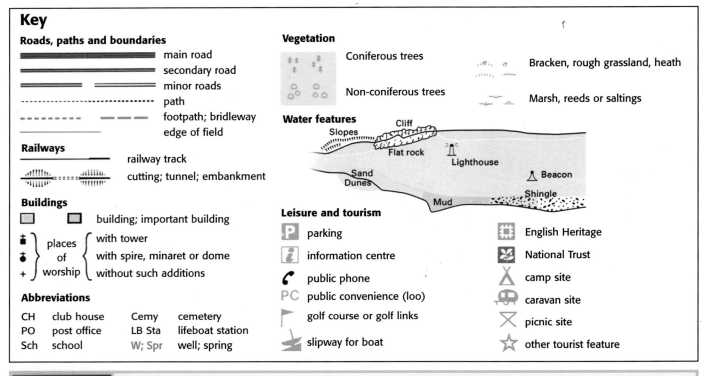

Key

Roads, paths and boundaries

main road
secondary road
minor roads
path
footpath; bridleway
edge of field

Railways

railway track
cutting; tunnel; embankment

Buildings

building; important building

places of worship:
with tower
with spire, minaret or dome
without such additions

Abbreviations

CH	club house	Cemy	cemetery
PO	post office	LB Sta	lifeboat station
Sch	school	W; Spr	well; spring

Vegetation

Coniferous trees

Non-coniferous trees

Bracken, rough grassland, heath

Marsh, reeds or saltings

Water features

Slopes, Cliff, Flat rock, Lighthouse, Sand Dunes, Mud, Shingle, Beacon

Leisure and tourism

P parking
i information centre
public phone
PC public convenience (loo)
golf course or golf links
slipway for boat

English Heritage
National Trust
camp site
caravan site
picnic site
other tourist feature

Your turn

1 Look at Warkworth on the OS map. Name the river that flows through it. Where is it flowing to?

2 What signs can you find that Warkworth is a historic place? List them. (There are three!)

3 What is at this grid reference, in Warkworth?
   a 247057   b 247062
   c 249063   d 247052

4 The top of an OS map is always north. Look back at the photo of Warkworth on page 20. Where on the photo is north?

5 There's a small yellow dot in the lower right corner of the photo on page 20. It marks the house where Walter's cousin Violet lives. Find her house on the OS map and write a six-figure grid reference for it.

6 Warkworth has a population of 1600. Now look at Amble. It has a population of:
   a 1000   b 2000   c 5600   d 9300
   How did you decide?

7 How many of these are there in Amble?
   a schools   b places of worship   c cemeteries

8 Find one of these on the map and give a six-figure grid reference for it:
   a a post office   b a club house
   c a public phone box   d a mast

9 What clues are there on the map that Warkworth and Amble get lots of visitors? Give as many as you can.

10 What is there for tourists to do, around Warkworth and Amble? Using the information on the map, write a list.

11 On the map, what clues are there that the coast and sea around Amble might be dangerous?

12 Violet used to go to the school in square 2503.
   a How far is it from her home? (Use the scale.)
   b Pretend you are Violet. Draw a sketch map of your route to the school. Mark in what you think are the key things you see on the way.

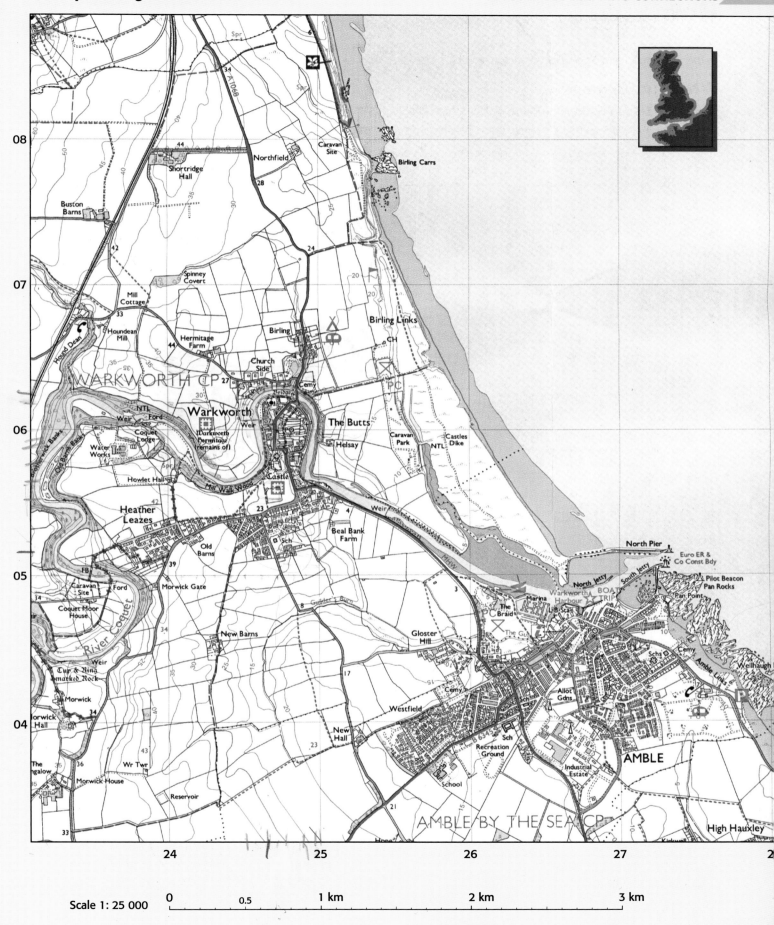

Scale 1: 25 000

0   0.5   1 km   2 km   3 km

How high?

In this unit you'll learn how height is shown on an OS map.

A hilly problem

This is the area in Cornwall where Walter's uncle lives. It's a little hilly.

Great Skewes

The same area is shown inside the red rectangle on the OS map below.

So how do you show on a map that an area is hilly? And how do you show how high it is? The OS map solves the problem in two ways …

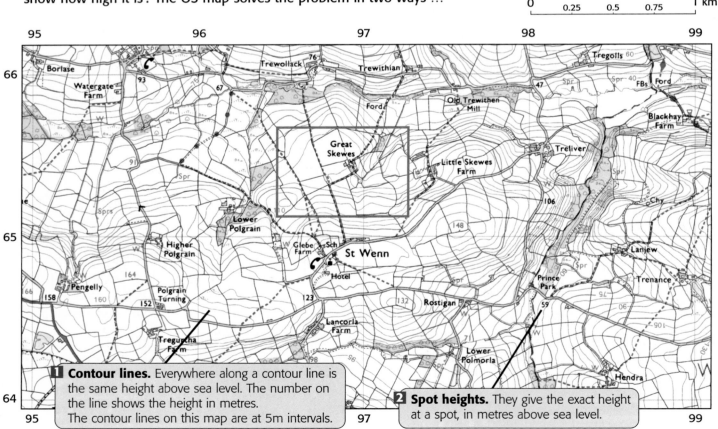

1 Contour lines. Everywhere along a contour line is the same height above sea level. The number on the line shows the height in metres.
The contour lines on this map are at 5m intervals.

2 Spot heights. They give the exact height at a spot, in metres above sea level.

More about contour lines

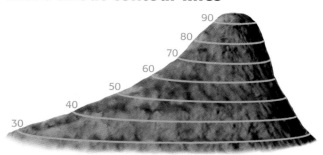

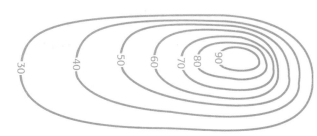

The contour lines are marked on this hill at 10 metre intervals. On a map, you see them from above …

… like this. They are close together where the slope is steep, and further apart where it is gentle.

> **Remember:**
> ◆ where contour lines are very far apart, it means the ground is flat.
> ◆ where they are very close together, the ground slopes steeply.

Did you know?
◆ *The highest place in the UK is Ben Nevis in Scotland.*
◆ *Some places in the UK are below sea level!*
(Check the map on page 127.)

Your turn

1 Match the drawings to the contour lines.
Start your answer like this: A =

A

1

B

2

C

3

The following questions refer to the map on page 24.

2 First, the map has lots of short crooked black lines everywhere. What do you think they show?

3 Find the contour line in the bottom right corner.
  a It is labelled 130. What does that mean?
  b What height does the line beside it represent?

4 About how high above sea level is:
  a Lancorla Farm (9664)?
  b Polgrain Turning (9564)?
  c Little Skewes Farm (9765)?
  d Lanjew (9864)?

5 a Which square has the steepest land? How can you tell?
  b Which square has most flat land? Did you have any problem deciding?

6 Find the highest point on the map and give a six-figure grid reference for it.

7 Going by road or track, say whether it is uphill, downhill or along flat land:
  a from Hendra (984642) to the road junction at 983645.
  b from Lancorla Farm (967644) into St Wenn (967648)
  c from Treliver (981655) to Little Skewes Farm (974654)
  d from Treliver (981655) to Old Trewithen Mill (975658)

8 You run a walking club. Your task is to plan an interesting walk in the area shown on the map.
  ◆ It must be *at least* 5 km long. (State the length.)
  ◆ You must keep to roads, tracks and footpaths.
  ◆ It must have variety!
  a Plan your route and draw a sketch map of it. Mark in features such as farms, woods and streams along the way.
  b For each part of the route, mark on your map whether it is uphill, downhill or along flat land. (You could show this using different colours.)
  c Add any spot heights for your route.
  d Give your map a title and a north arrow, and indicate whether it is to scale or not.

The big picture

This chapter is about settlements – the villages and towns and cities we live in.

These are the big ideas behind the chapter:

◆ Humans like us first appeared on the Earth about 200 000 years ago, and began to spread all over it.

◆ As they explored it, they found places they wanted to settle in.

◆ They started by building shelters. Over time, these grew into villages, and towns, and cities.

◆ Today, many of our settlements are still growing – and we're still building shelters. (We call them houses!)

Your goals for this chapter

By the end of this chapter you should be able to answer these questions:

◆ What factors did our ancestors think about, in choosing a place to settle in?

◆ What do these terms mean?

settlement   site   situation

◆ What kinds of things cause a settlement to grow?

◆ What is the settlement hierarchy, and what does a diagram of it look like?

◆ What patterns of land use am I likely to find in a British town or city? And how did these patterns come about?

◆ What can an OS map tell me, about land use in a town or city?

◆ What do these terms mean?

urban area   rural area   redevelopment
urban regeneration   greenfield   brownfield

◆ In what ways might land use change over time?

◆ What does *a sustainable way of life* mean, and what examples can I give?

◆ Why does the UK need more houses, and what kinds of conflict does this cause?

And then …

When you finish the chapter, come back to this page and see if you have met your goals!

Did you know?

◆ The remains of a house nearly 10 000 years old were found in Northumberland.
◆ It's a shallow pit, which still had traces of ancient meals (including nutshells)!

Did you know?

◆ By 2004, 24 of the world's cities had over 10 million people each!

Did you know?

◆ The settlement called London was started by the Romans, around 50 AD.
◆ We think its name means 'the settlement on the wide river.'

Your chapter starter

Page 26 shows a settlement.

What's a settlement?

Pick out five key things you notice about this one.

Do you think it has always looked like this? Give your reasons.

In what ways is your settlement like this one? In what ways is it different?

Settle down, you lot!

Settling down

In this unit you'll find out what we humans looked for, when choosing a place to settle in.

Once upon a time

The Earth was empty for billions of years. But life evolved. And around 200 000 years ago …

… the first humans appeared. They lived by eating fruit and berries, and hunting …

… which meant they were nearly always on the move, chasing dinner.

Then, one day, they noticed something amazing: where they dropped seeds, plants grew!

So they began to settle down in one place and grow their food. These were the first farmers.

They chose a place or **site** that had what they needed. Like good flat land … water … wood for fuel …

… shelter from wind and rain … materials for making things (clay, sand, iron ore, tin …) …

… easy access to other places for trading … and protection from their enemies.

They cleared the land and planted crops and put up dwellings. The result – a **settlement**.

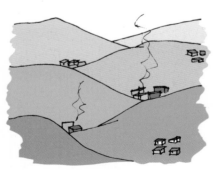

Years passed. The numbers of humans – and settlements – grew.

Some settlements grew larger and larger. And now …

… there are over 6 billion humans, and half of us live in cities.

Your turn

1 It is 5000 BC. You are leading your tribe on a search for a place to settle in. Draw a spider map showing the factors you will consider, when choosing a site – like this:

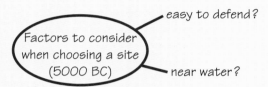

easy to defend?

Factors to consider when choosing a site (5000 BC)

near water?

2 Copy and complete in your own words:
   a A settlement is …
   b A site is …
   c The *situation* of a settlement means …
   The glossary may help.

3 Look at the photos A to E. For each photo, decide whether it shows a settlement or not. Give your reasons.

4 For each *settlement* in the photos, suggest reasons for choosing that site. (Try for at least two reasons for each.)

5 The five photos were taken in the countries listed below. Try to match each photo to the correct country.
Switzerland   Morocco   The Philippines
France   Canada

6 The government wants to build a new town in the UK, starting next year.
   a What factors do you think will be important, when choosing a site for it? List them, and say why they are important.
   b Underline any factors that did *not* apply in 5000 BC.

Example: settling in Aylesbury

In this unit you'll find out who settled first in Aylesbury – and why.

Once upon a time

7000 years ago, Great Britain was covered in thick forest. Only small groups of hunters lived here.

Then, around 6000 years ago, farmers arrived from mainland Europe. They brought animals, seeds and ploughs. They cleared land and started farming.

As time passed they were joined by many other groups. Look at the table on the right.

The new arrivals

Who?	Around when?	From where?
Early farmers	4000 BC	The continent
Celts	800 BC	Central Europe
Romans	40 AD	Italy
Saxons	500 AD	Germany
Vikings	850 AD	Norway, Denmark
Normans	1066 AD	France

So who settled in Aylesbury?

Aylesbury is a town about 55 km from London. It lies in the middle of Aylesbury Vale, a large stretch of good farmland.

We know the Celts and Romans spent some time here. But the first people to really settle here were the Saxons.

This sketch map shows what they would have found when they arrived, around 1500 years ago.

Key

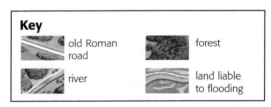

old Roman road

river

forest

land liable to flooding

easy to cross river here

raised well-drained outcrop of limestone

remains of Celtic hill fort

X

Y

to London ▶

flat land, clay soil, good for farming

0   1km

Creating a settlement

The Saxons built their huts in groups. Each group of huts held an extended family (granny, uncles, cousins …). They often built a larger hut in the middle of the group, where the family met to eat and talk.

Over time, the Saxons became Christian and built churches too.

▲ Saxon homes – reconstructed in West Stow Anglo-Saxon Village, Suffolk.

Then and now

Below is how a map of Aylesbury may have looked, in the year 700.

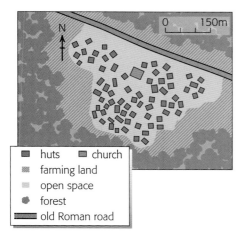

■ huts	■ church
▨ farming land	
▭ open space	
♣ forest	
▬ old Roman road	

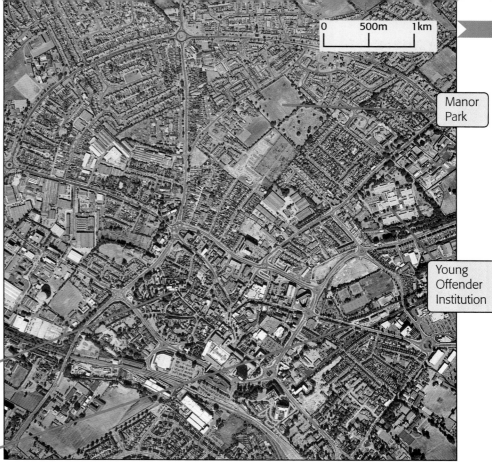

Manor Park

Young Offender Institution

The 13th century church here is built on the site of an early Saxon church …
… which in turn was built on the site of the Celtic hill fort.

The Roman road to London is now the A41.

This shows just *part* of Aylesbury today. It has grown rather a lot!
Look at the OS map on page 35, and check for the things noted above.

Your turn

1 You are a Saxon. Your group will start a settlement at **X**, **Y**, or **Z** on the map on page 30. It's time to choose!
   a First, make a table like this one.

Factors to consider	Site X	Site Y	Site Z
access to water			
access to timber			
access to farmland			
access to other places			
ease of defence			
safe from flooding			
Total score			

   b Now give each site a score of 1 − 5 for each factor. (1 = poor, 5 = excellent.)
   c Add up the total scores for each site.
   d Which site seems the best choice, to you?

2 In fact your leader decides on site **X**. So what do you think is his main worry, about life in Britain?

3 **X** was a good choice, and Aylesbury grew a lot. The OS map on page 35 shows the town today. Which of the above factors might still be important for the people who live there now? Give reasons.

4 Settlements are all different shapes. Look at these:

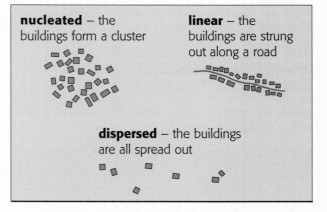

nucleated – the buildings form a cluster

linear – the buildings are strung out along a road

dispersed – the buildings are all spread out

   a Which shape is the early Saxon settlement at the top of this page?
   b Which term would you use for Aylesbury today?

5 Look again at the OS map on page 35. Which of the above terms would you use for:
   a Weston Turville (8510)? b Bishopstone (8010)?
   c Kimble Wick (8007)?   d Halton (8710)?

6 Finally, a challenge. See if you can explain *why* settlements took on the different shapes above.

How settlements grow

In this unit you'll learn how and why some settlements grow.

A good choice?

In the last two units you saw how new arrivals chose a place to settle.
If the site is a good one, the settlement will grow. Like this …

I hear they be needin' a good baker.

Good gracious, wife!

And next I'm going to build a factory round it.

But it's only steam, Silas!

Will they give us lunch?

People hear it's a good place, and come looking for work – for example as bakers and carpenters.

The population also grows naturally – but quite slowly – through birth.

But around 1750, the Industrial Revolution arrives. And from now on, many settlements …

… grow rapidly, because people flock in from the countryside to work in the new factories.

AD 600   **1000**   **1800**

In this way, small settlements grew into villages, then towns, then cities.
As they grew they took over the countryside or **rural areas** around them.
This process is called **urbanisation**. (**Urban** means *built up*.)

Example: Aylesbury

On page 30 you saw how the Saxons settled at Aylesbury.

The land was good. The site was easy to get to. So farmers and craftsmen from miles around brought their goods there, to sell.

Aylesbury became a market town. It grew and grew. Compare these two maps:

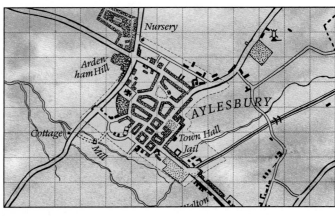

▲ Map of Aylesbury, 1830.

0   0.5   1 km

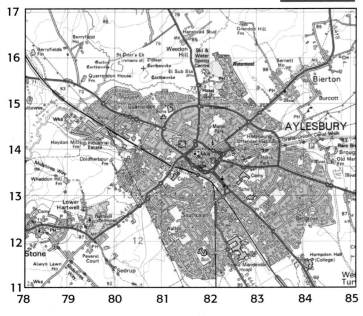

▲ Map of Aylesbury, 2002.

0   0.5   1 km

Aylesbury since 1810

Aylesbury is still a market town, but now it has many businesses.
Table 1 shows how the population has grown since 1810.
Table 2 shows events that helped Aylesbury to grow.

Table 1

How many people live in Aylesbury?

Year	Population
1810	3400
1830	5000
1850	6000
1870	6900
1890	8900
1910	11 000
1930	14 400
1950	21 200
1970	40 500
1990	51 000
2005	65 200
2010	?

Table 2 Some events that helped Aylesbury to grow

Year	Event
1814	Grand Union Canal links Aylesbury to London and other places.
1839	Birmingham Railway links it to Birmingham.
1865	Hazel, Watson and Vine, printers from London, set up a factory.
1870	Aylesbury Condensed Milk Company starts. It is now Nestles.
1892	Metropolitan Railway links Aylesbury to London.
1960	New council houses being built, to take overspill from London.
1988	Sony Music sets up factory.
1991	New shopping centre opened, called Friar's Square.

Your turn

1

a This shot was taken in Aylesbury. What's going on?
b How and when do you think this tradition started?
c How do you think it has changed over the years?
d Now see if you can locate the site on the map on
   page 35, and give a 6-figure grid reference. (Spire?)

2 Look at the map of Aylesbury for 1830. Each square
   represents 0.25 square kilometres. You can work out
   the area roughly, by counting squares like this:

Full = 1.   At least half full = 1.   Less than half full = 0.
About what area did Aylesbury cover in 1830?

3 Now look at the map for 2002. Here each square
   represents 1 square kilometre.
   a About what area did Aylesbury cover in 2002?
   b About how many times larger was it in 2002
      than in 1830? (Divide the area in 2002 by the
      area in 1830.)

4 a What was the population of Aylesbury in 1830?
   b How many times larger had it grown by 2005?

5 A graph will help you see how fast the population
   of Aylesbury has grown.

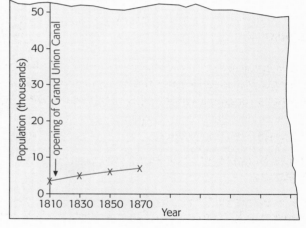

a Draw a graph like the one started here, for Table 1.
   Use a whole page, and complete both axes.
b If the population keeps growing like this, what will it
   be in 2010? Show this on your graph.
c Now mark in all the events from Table 2.

6 Suggest a reason why:
   a the canal helped Aylesbury to grow
   b condensed milk was made in Aylesbury
   c the railway to London has helped it to grow
   d Friar's Square shopping centre is helping it to grow.

7 Draw a spider map to show
   factors that help towns
   keep on growing.
   Think of as many as
   you can (not just the
   ones mentioned in
   this unit).

Factors that help towns grow — Good road and rail links — Good shops

The settlement hierarchy

In this unit you will learn how settlements can be ranked in order of size and importance.

From little to large

Some settlements are only tiny. Some are large and lively with a whole range of services. Look at these examples:

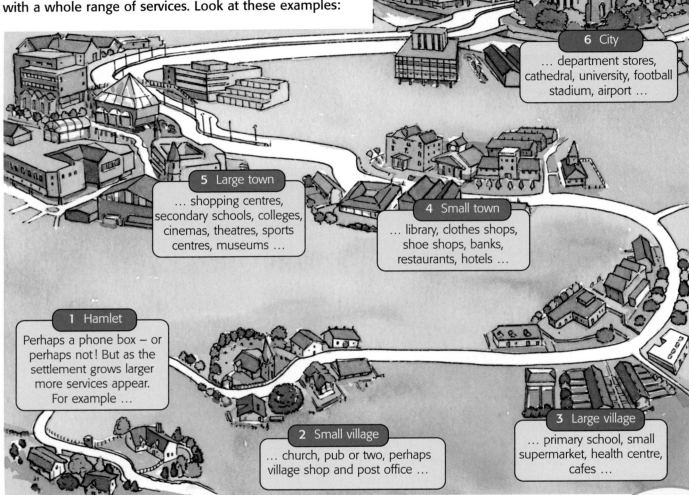

6 City
… department stores, cathedral, university, football stadium, airport …

5 Large town
… shopping centres, secondary schools, colleges, cinemas, theatres, sports centres, museums …

4 Small town
… library, clothes shops, shoe shops, banks, restaurants, hotels …

1 Hamlet
Perhaps a phone box – or perhaps not! But as the settlement grows larger more services appear. For example …

2 Small village
… church, pub or two, perhaps village shop and post office …

3 Large village
… primary school, small supermarket, health centre, cafes …

Did you know?
- Lots of small villages in the UK now have **no** shops.
- They closed because they did not get enough customers.

Ranking settlements

We can rank settlements in order of size and importance. A ranking like this is called a **hierarchy**:

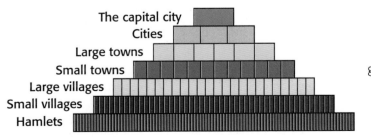

The capital city
Cities
Large towns
Small towns
Large villages
Small villages
Hamlets

As settlements get larger they offer more services.

There are far more hamlets than towns or cities.

You can guess from an OS map where a settlement fits in the hierarchy. Larger settlements take more space on the map, and show more services!

Your turn   OS map of Aylesbury area

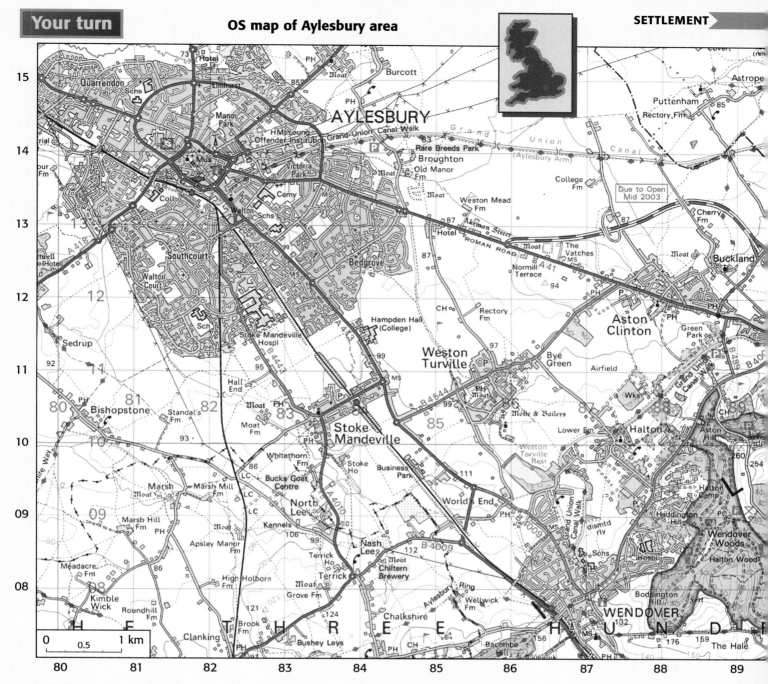

1 The larger a settlement, the more services it offers.
  a What is a *service*? (Try the glossary.)
  b Give five examples of services.

2 a Make a *large* table with headings like this:

Settlement	Services shown	Population	Type of settlement
Bishopstone	1 church		

  b In your table, list *all* the services the map above shows, for Bishopstone. (Page 126 will help.)
  c Now add these settlements, and their services:
    Aston Clinton   Aylesbury   Marsh   Wendover

3 The populations of the five settlements are roughly:
    3540   7620   290   50   65 170
  Write each in the *correct* place in the table.

4 Each settlement is a different type. For example only one is a small village. In the last column of your table, name the type of settlement. (The size of the writing used for its name on the map is an extra clue!)

5 Now look at the roads to (or through) the five settlements. Can you find a link between the size of a settlement and the number and type of roads? Describe what you find.

6 a Look at the statement in this triangle. Is it true? See if you can prove it, using the map above.
  b What (if anything) did you find difficult about a?

There are fewer settlements at each level, as you go up the hierarchy.

Patterns of land use in towns and cities

In this unit you'll learn that factories, houses and offices are not all jumbled up together in a town or city. There is a pattern to it ...

How the pattern grew

- ◆ A settlement usually grows out from the centre. So that's where the oldest buildings are.
- ◆ As the settlement grew, homes in the centre were turned into shops and offices, that people could reach easily from all directions.
- ◆ So the main shops and offices are still in the centre. It's called the **central business district** or **CBD**.
- ◆ The first factories were built along canals, rivers or railways, so that goods could be moved easily.
- ◆ Rows of small cheap terraced houses were built close to the factories, for the workers.
- ◆ As the population grew, new houses were built at the edges of the settlement, where land was cheaper.
- ◆ Today, new industries are usually set up close to major roads, towards the edge of town.

An urban model

We can show the pattern using a **model** – a simplified picture.

On the right is one model. No town or city is *exactly* like this model. For example in real life the CBD is never a neat circle! But many fit it quite well.

New industrial area
Industrial estates and business parks built since 1970, close to main roads.

Old industrial area
Along a river, canal or railway. Many old factories now closed. Area may look run down.

Modern housing
New houses and housing estates. New shopping centres. Parks and other open areas. This area is the **outer suburbs**.

Housing 1920–1950
Larger houses usually with gardens. Some parks. Some rows of shops. This area is the **inner suburbs**.

19th century housing
Mostly terraced houses for factory workers. Some now replaced by high-rise flats. Small corner shops nearby. This area is the **inner city** or **transition zone**.

The CBD
Large shops and offices. Restaurants, cafes, museums, cinemas and theatres.

In general, as you move out from the CBD:
- ◆ land gets cheaper to buy or rent
- ◆ housing gets more modern.

Your turn

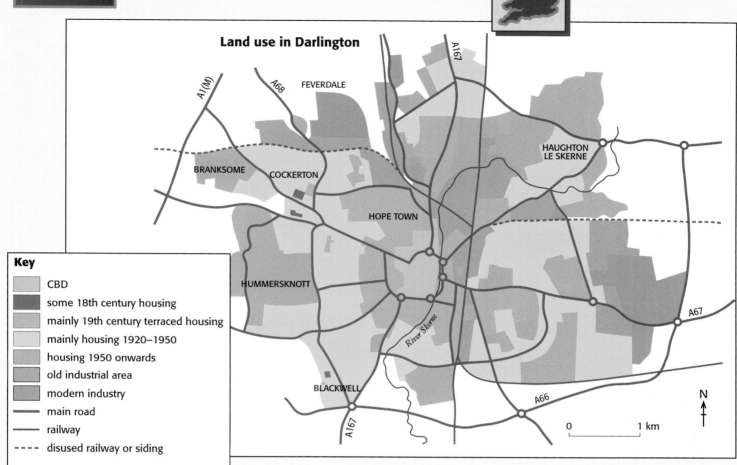

Land use in Darlington

Key
- CBD
- some 18th century housing
- mainly 19th century terraced housing
- mainly housing 1920–1950
- housing 1950 onwards
- old industrial area
- modern industry
- —— main road
- —— railway
- ---- disused railway or siding

1 Above is a map of Darlington in County Durham.
  It does not look much like our model!
  But let's see how it matches it.
  Say whether each statement is true or false.
  a The CBD is roughly in the centre of Darlington.
  b Most of the terraced housing is around the centre.
  c Most of the modern housing is built towards the edges of the town.
  d The early factories were built as far as possible from the railway.

2 Here are two Darlington houses. One is in Hope Town, the other in Cockerton. Which is which?

3 Why were the terraced houses built where they are?

4 The map shows some 18th century housing. Give a reason why it is located here. (Think about how the town grew!)

5 There is some modern housing close to the CBD.
  a How do you think it came to be here?
  b Think of two advantages of living in this housing.

6 Look for the modern industry in the Feverdale area. Now give two reasons why it is located here.

7 The map shows just the main roads (not all the streets.) Look at the road pattern.
  a Many roads head towards the CBD.
    i How does this help the CBD?
    ii What problems might it cause?
  b In the centre, a road loops around a large part of the CBD. Why do you think this was built?

8 Finally, see if you can explain why:
  a large department stores are found in the CBD.
  b it costs more to rent a shop in the CBD than in a modern shopping centre on the edge of town.
  c buildings in the CBD are often several storeys high.

Be a land-use detective!

In this unit you'll learn how to identify different types of land use, on an OS map of a town or city.

What clues should you look for?

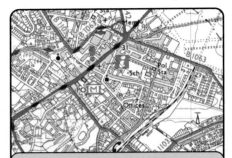

The central business district
Look for these clues:
- main roads coming together
- may have an inner ring road
- has things like churches, a hospital, cathedral, museum, tourist information centre.

An area of 19th century workers' housing
Look for these clues:
- straight rows of small houses (as in the photo above)
- streets close together
- little or no green space
- often near factory, railway, canal.

An area of 1920–1950 housing
Look for these clues:
- houses usually have gardens (see the tiny white rectangles)
- streets usually quite straight
- schools and parks nearby.

An old industrial area
Look for these clues:
- often along river, railway or canal
- large buildings
- factory may be shown as 'Works'.

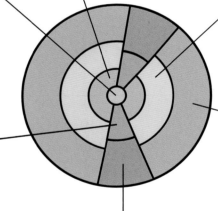

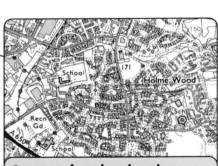

An area of modern housing
Look for these clues:
- further from the CBD
- houses usually have gardens
- houses often in small groups (as in the photo below)
- schools and parks nearby.

A new industrial area
Look for these clues:
- labels like 'Industrial Estate' or 'Ind Est' or 'Science Park'
- towards the edge of town
- usually close to main roads.

OS map of Darlington 1:25 000

1 The OS map above shows most of Darlington. Most of the CBD lies in one square on the map.
   a Using page 38 to help you, find the CBD.
   b Give a four-figure grid reference for the square that contains most of it.
   c What clues tell you that this is the CBD?

2 Look at the houses to the north of the hospital, in square 2815. When do you think they were built? Use page 38 to help you decide, and give evidence for your answer.

3 You work on the trading estate in 2915. You want to buy a modern house, with plenty of space around it, and as close to work as possible. There are four houses for sale, at these grid references:
   A 308170   B 294164   C 291163   D 312155
   a Which house is most likely to meet your needs?
   b Explain why you rejected each of the others.

4 Square 2816 is largely an industrial area. Is it an old industrial area, or a new one? Give evidence.

5 Most of the land in Darlington is used for houses, industry, shops and offices. But some is used for roads, and farming, and other things.
   a Make a table with these headings:

Other types of land use in Darlington		
transport	leisure	other
roads		

   b In your table, write in all the other types of land use you can find on the map.

6 a Now, choose any square on the map, and draw a spider map to show all the types of land use in it.
   b When you have finished, swop spider maps with a partner, and try to identify each other's squares!

39

In this unit you'll see an example of how land use changes over time.

The history of Greenwich Peninsula

In any town or city, land use changes over time. For example an old factory may get pulled down to make way for new homes or offices. Greenwich Peninsula in London has seen big changes.

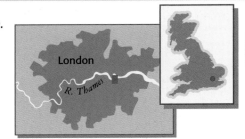
London
R. Thames

By 1800, Greenwich Peninsula was still a rural area. Around 500 people lived there. Some had market gardens where they grew vegetables to sell in London.

By 1860 industry had arrived: shipyards to build ships, and factories to make rope, chemicals, soap, ammunition and ice. In 1889 a huge gas works opened, making gas from coal.

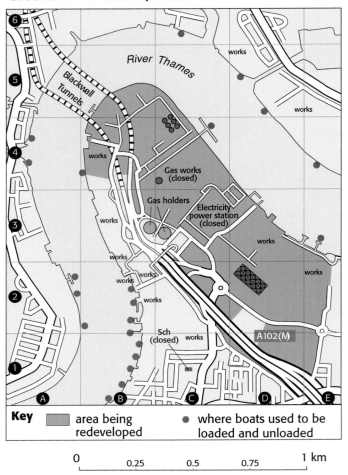

Greenwich Peninsula, 1995

River Thames
Blackwall Tunnels
works
Gas works (closed)
Gas holders
Electricity power station (closed)
works
Sch (closed)
A102(M)

Key
— area being redeveloped
● where boats used to be loaded and unloaded

0   0.25   0.5   0.75   1 km

But one by one, the old industries closed down. The gas works closed in 1985 because we switched to North Sea gas. Much of the area became **derelict**.

Today it has a new life. The Millennium Dome is just one of the new buildings on the old gasworks site. The whole area is being **redeveloped**.

The redevelopment

Work began in 1997 and will go on until 2025.

The plan is to provide 13 000 new homes – plus offices, shops, hotels, cinemas, restaurants, a health centre, and two schools. (Some have been built already.)

There will also be parks to relax in, and walking trails, and bike tracks, and ducks to feed.

By 2025, it is hoped that there will be 30 000 jobs on the peninsula.

The redevelopment plan

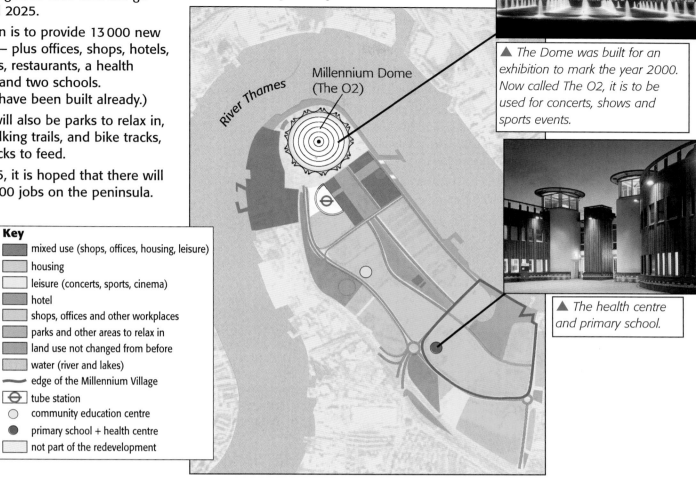

Millennium Dome (The O2)

River Thames

Key

▨	mixed use (shops, offices, housing, leisure)
▢	housing
▢	leisure (concerts, sports, cinema)
▨	hotel
▨	shops, offices and other workplaces
▨	parks and other areas to relax in
▨	land use not changed from before
▢	water (river and lakes)
⌒	edge of the Millennium Village
⊖	tube station
○	community education centre
●	primary school + health centre
▢	not part of the redevelopment

▲ The Dome was built for an exhibition to mark the year 2000. Now called The O2, it is to be used for concerts, shows and sports events.

▲ The health centre and primary school.

Your turn

1 Look at the map of the Greenwich Peninsula on page 40. Why is it called a peninsula? (Try the glossary?)

2 Over the years, there have been big changes in what the land is used for, on Greenwich Peninsula. Using the images on these pages to help you, describe the land use there in each of these years:
  a 1800   b 1860   c 1995   d 2025
  Write one paragraph for each year.

3 Look again at the map on page 40.
  a What signs of industry can you see on it?
  b Suggest reasons why factories started up in this area. Think of as many as you can.

4 a The area was *derelict*, and is being *redeveloped*. Write the above sentence in words that an 8-year-old could understand.
  b Give one reason to explain why the area became derelict.

5 Before redeveloping the area, a layer of soil up to 1.2 m thick had to be removed, cleaned and put back again. (That cost a fortune to do.) Why did it need cleaning?

6 Copy and complete:
  Greenwich Peninsula is a good example of ur_____ reg ____ . (Glossary!)

7 You run a small design company with 6 staff, near Greenwich Peninsula. You plan to move your office to the location marked ● on the map above. Write a memo to your staff telling them about your plan, and the new office, and why you think they will like it there.

8 'The redevelopment of Greenwich Peninsula is a waste of money'. Do you agree with this statement? Decide what *you* think, and write a speech in reply.

41

Is this the future?

In this unit you'll learn how Greenwich Peninsula aims to set a good example !

A sustainable way of life

If something is **sustainable**, that means it does not waste things, or harm people, or the environment.

In most settlements we waste energy, and water. We have traffic jams, and fill the air with fumes. People can feel really isolated. And only rich people can afford the nicer areas.

Greenwich Peninsula aims to show us a more sustainable way to live. Like this …

Saving water

1 The rain falling on the roof of The O2 is used for the toilets.

2 The rain falling on the supermarket roof is used to water plants.

3 Waste water from baths, showers and wash basins in Village homes is filtered and used to flush toilets and water plants.

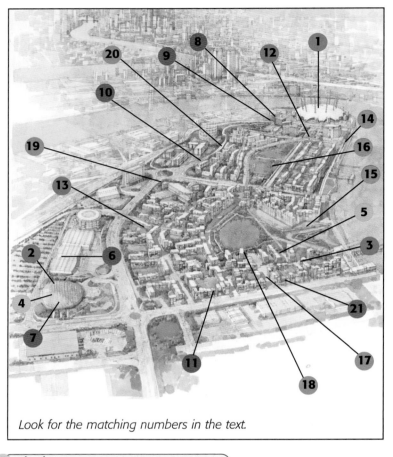

Look for the matching numbers in the text.

Saving energy

4 Supermarkets use electricity for light and heat and fridges. This one aims to save electricity. It:

- makes some of its own, using **wind power** and **solar power** (sunlight).
- has banks of earth on each side to keep it warm in winter and cool in summer.
- has a glass roof to let light in.

Look at the photo below.

5 The houses:

- are built using methods that save energy and materials.
- are well **insulated** to keep heat in.
- are sheltered from cold winds.
- have south-facing glass walls to trap the sun's heat.
- have energy-saving fridges, washing machines and dishwashers.

Cutting traffic

Cars jam streets, and cause pollution. So people living here are encouraged not to drive.

6 You can walk to the shops, and schools – and to work if you get a local job.

7 You can order from the supermarket by internet, and have your shopping delivered.

8 There is a tube station right beside The O2.

9 There is a very good bus service.

10 There are lots of cycle tracks.

11 There are fewer parking spaces than homes – and they are hidden from view.

Recycling material

12 The building materials can all be **recycled** (used again).

13 Used bottles, cans, plastic and paper are collected for recycling.

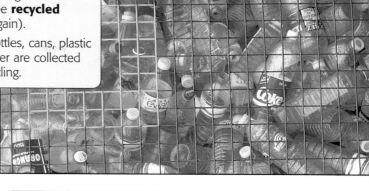

Attracting wildlife

14 Reed beds and salt marshes are being created along the river, to attract ducks and other birds.

15 There are large stretches of park, with lakes and ponds.

16 Over 12 000 trees are being planted.

Building a community

17 You can rent or buy a house. And almost 40% of the houses will be lower cost.

18 The footpaths and open spaces help you meet your neighbours.

19 The health centre is next to the primary school – handy for mums.

20 The community education centre will run classes for all ages.

Using technology

21 The houses are really hi-tech!

◆ They all have computers.

◆ These link them to the Village website, and the school and health centre.

◆ Their fire alarms are linked to a local fire station.

◆ Their burglar alarms are linked to a security centre.

Your turn

1 Do you think Greenwich Peninsula would suit:

a an old person living alone?

b a family with two young children?

c you?

Give reasons for each answer. (Draw spider maps?)

2 What does *a sustainable way of life* mean?

3 a Draw a table like the one started on the right.

b Now choose the five features of Greenwich Peninsula that you think are the *most important*, for a sustainable way of life. (For example, how important is it to be able to walk to the shops?) Don't forget features that make people feel good.

c Write the features in column one of your table.

d In column two, list the benefits of each feature.

e Now look at the benefits. Underline any *social* benefits in one colour, *economic* benefits in another, and *environmental* benefits in a third. (Glossary?) Add a key below your table to explain the colours.

4 Now think about *your* local area. Does it help to promote a sustainable way of life? Give evidence (examples) for your answer.

Top 5 features of Greenwich Peninsula, for a sustainable way of life	
Feature	Benefits
....	....
	....

Help! We need more homes

In this unit you will explore the reasons why the UK needs more homes – and the conflicts over where to put them.

Bring on the builders!

Today the government published a new report on housing in the UK. And the message is: we need lots more houses – and fast! We need at least 195 000 new homes a year, including low-cost homes for people on low incomes.

If we don't speed up our house building, more and more people will end up in 'bed-and-breakfast' accommodation, or even on the streets. And house prices will rocket, as buyers compete for too few homes.

195 000 ! That's a lot of houses ! So get ready for the sight of builders' trucks, and the sound of hammering, all over the UK.

Adapted from newspaper reports, 17 March 2004.

So where should the new homes go?

There is a great deal of argument about where to put the new houses.

A

We could build them on **greenfield sites**. These are sites which have not been built on before. Like the one shown here, out in a rural area.

B

Or on **brownfield sites**. These are sites that were already built on, but are now derelict. Like this waste ground in a city.

C

Here's what the site above looks like now, with a new housing estate built on it. (Match the roundabout.)

D

Here's what the site above looked like, with new houses being built on it. (Match the blue dots.)

Your turn

1 Why do we need more houses in the UK?
Each drawing above shows one reason!

a Work out what each drawing is saying, and then give that reason in words.

b Now see if you can think of any other reasons.

2 There is a lot of argument about *where* new homes should go. Look at these four people:

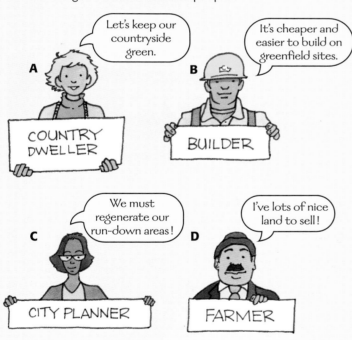

a In this group, who is **A** likely to be in conflict with?

b Who is likely to take sides with **A**, but for a different reason?

c Which two might get on really well together?

3 Now compare sites A and B on page 44.

a Which do you think is a *wiser* choice for new homes? Give your reasons.

b Where would *you* prefer to live – at C or at D? Why?

Pros and cons

A It will mean more traffic on country roads.

B New major roads will need to be built.

C Lots of wildlife will be driven away.

D It will mean less peace in the countryside.

E Nice green views will get ruined.

F The area will look better.

G There will be less land for farming.

H More shops and schools may be needed, for the people who move there.

I It's a good use of waste ground.

J More countryside will get covered in concrete.

K It will bring a dead area back to life.

L Traffic jams in the city may get worse.

M Trees will probably have to be cut down.

N It means more household rubbish to get rid of.

---

4 Look at statements **A** to **N** above.
They include **pros** (good points) and **cons** (bad points) about using the two types of site.
But they are all mixed up.

a First, make a larger copy of this Venn diagram.

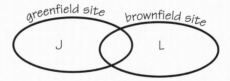

b Next write the letters A to N in the correct place in your diagram. (J and L have been done.)
If you think a letter applies to both kinds of site, write it in the middle.

c Now underline all the 'pro' letters in one colour. Do the 'con' letters in another colour.
(Some statements might not be either.)

d Which type of site has more pros?

5 There are about 750 000 empty houses in the UK, at any one time. And there are many large houses with just one person.
You are the government minister in charge of housing. Look at these suggestions:

Would it be *fair* to do these things?
Write down what you will say to each person in reply.

Changing the way we shop

The big picture

This chapter is about shopping – where we buy what, and how shopping is changing. These are the big ideas behind the chapter:

◆ Shopping is all tied up with geography !

◆ We're willing to travel further for some goods than others.

◆ Shops need to be located where they'll get enough customers to make a profit.

◆ Shopping is always changing. Out-of-town shopping and internet shopping are examples of changes.

Your goals for this chapter

By the end of this chapter you should be able to answer these questions:

◆ What are convenience goods ?

◆ What are comparison goods ?

◆ For which of those goods are people willing to travel further ?

◆ Why do shops set up in some places – and not others ?

◆ Why do bigger settlements have a larger range of shops than small settlements do ?

◆ What is an out-of-town shopping centre, and what am I likely to find there ?

◆ Who may benefit from out-of-town shopping – and who may lose out ?

◆ How does internet shopping work ?

◆ Who may benefit from internet shopping – and who may lose out ?

And then …

When you finish the chapter, come back to this page and see if you have met your goals !

Did you know?
◆ Until the 17th century, most 'shops' were market stalls.

Did you know?
◆ 200 years ago, your clothes would have been sewn by hand …
◆ … because sewing machines were not invented until around 1850.

Did you know?
◆ Factory-made clothes didn't hit the shops in a big way until around 1950.
◆ Up till then, tailors and dressmakers were kept busy.

Did you know?
◆ Over 13 000 specialist shops in the UK (such as butchers and bakers) closed in the five years up to 2002.

Your chapter starter

Look at the first photo on page 46. That's the shop owner at the door, with the tape measure around his neck.

About how many years ago do you think the photo was taken:
30?   60?   100?   120?   180?

What do you think shopping would have been like, in that shop ?

In what ways would it have been different from shopping in the other shop ?

Do I look good in this?

Shopping around

In this unit you'll learn why shops are where they are – and see how shopping is all tied up with geography!

Just good fun?

Shopping can be fun. But behind the fun is some very serious business!

There is a pattern to where shops are located, and where we go for different things. And this pattern is the result of two key factors.

1 There are two types of goods

There are some things we buy often, or quite often, that don't cost much, and which we are happy to buy…

Then there are goods we don't need to buy so often, and that cost more. We like to compare styles and prices before we buy …

… in the nearest convenient place, for example the local corner shop. So they are called **convenience goods**.

… so they are called **comparison goods**. We are prepared to travel to get a good choice – for example into the town or city centre.

▲ *Oh go on then.*

2 Shops have to make a profit!

That'll be £3.60 please.

If you sell convenience goods, you can make a profit even in a village. Local people may call in several times a week.

But if you try to sell the latest fashions there, it's a different story. You won't get enough customers. Your business will fail.

You will need to move your clothing store to a place where there are lots of shoppers. For example into the next town.

So let's see how these factors affect you, when you go shopping!

Your turn

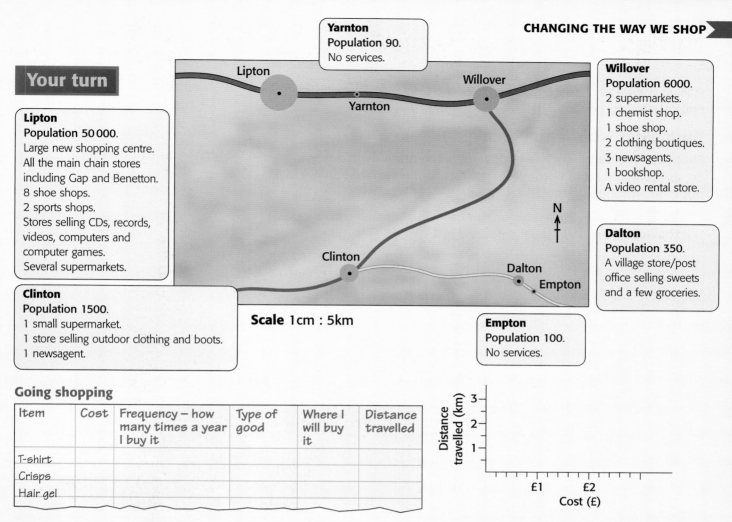

Yarnton
Population 90.
No services.

Lipton
Population 50 000.
Large new shopping centre.
All the main chain stores
including Gap and Benetton.
8 shoe shops.
2 sports shops.
Stores selling CDs, records,
videos, computers and
computer games.
Several supermarkets.

Willover
Population 6000.
2 supermarkets.
1 chemist shop.
1 shoe shop.
2 clothing boutiques.
3 newsagents.
1 bookshop.
A video rental store.

Dalton
Population 350.
A village store/post
office selling sweets
and a few groceries.

Clinton
Population 1500.
1 small supermarket.
1 store selling outdoor clothing and boots.
1 newsagent.

Empton
Population 100.
No services.

Scale 1cm : 5km

N

Going shopping

Item	Cost	Frequency – how many times a year I buy it	Type of good	Where I will buy it	Distance travelled
T-shirt					
Crisps					
Hair gel					

Distance travelled (km) / Cost (£)

Look at the map above. You live at Empton on it – and you are going shopping!

1 Look at the table started above. It shows items you might buy *at least once a year*.
  a Make your own table with the same headings, and ten rows to fill in.
  b In column 1, fill in ten items. Try for a mix of low-cost items and more expensive ones.
  c Write the cost of each item in column 2. If you are not sure, ask a friend, or guess.
  d Now fill in column 3.

2 a Explain in your own words what these terms mean:
    i convenience goods   ii comparison goods
  b Now, for each item in your table, write the correct term, *convenience* or *comparison*, in column 4.

3 Next, decide where to shop. You will make a separate trip for each item. (Not like real life!)
  a Start with the first item in your list. Where on the map will you buy it? (You may want a good choice, but at the same time you don't want to spend too much time or money travelling. You have to pay for any petrol!) Write your decision in column 5.
  b How far will you travel (*both ways*) for it? Measure along the road, from your Empton dot to the centre of the place, using a suitable method, and then use the scale. Write your answer in column 6.
  c Repeat a and b for the other items in your table.

4 Now you will draw a scattergram. You will plot the cost of items against the distance you're prepared to travel.
  a Draw the axes as shown in the diagram.
  b Mark the crosses for comparison goods in one colour, and convenience goods in another.
  c Describe any pattern you find, and then explain it.

5 a Look at the map again. Why is there:
    i no supermarket at Dalton?
    ii no video rental shop in Clinton?
  b Why have so many shops set up in Lipton?
  c Now write a general rule linking the size of a place with the number and range of shops in it.
    (It could start like this: *The larger a place is, the* ...)

6 The **sphere of influence** of a place means the area around it, that is affected by it. For example the area from which it attracts shoppers.
  a Which places on the map above do you think are in Lipton's sphere of influence?
  b Which are in Dalton's sphere of influence?

Out-of-town shopping: Bluewater

In this unit you'll learn about Europe's biggest out-of-town shopping centre, and explore its impact.

Bluewater – shopping heaven?

Shops want to be where lots of customers can reach them easily. So, as more and more households got cars, someone had a bright idea: out-of-town shopping centres!

These photos shows Bluewater, an out-of-town shopping centre in Kent. It is the largest one in Europe. It opened in 1999.

Things you can do there
- shopping, of course!
- eat and drink
- go to the cinema
- go boating and cycling
- play in the mini sports stadium
- cook, read, or play on a computer
- talk over your problems with a helper
- get help with homework

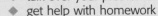

Outside
- six man-made lakes
- parks to walk in
- a water garden
- parking for 13 000 cars

Bluewater factfile
- It cost £350 million to build.
- It employs around 7000 people.
- At least one busload of shoppers arrives every minute.

Inside
- over 320 high-quality shops
- over 40 places to eat and drink
- a 13-screen cinema

Before
- Bluewater is built on the site of an old chalk quarry.

Bluewater on the map

Key

▬▬	motorway	△	Bluewater
──	main road	■	Lakeside shopping centre
──	secondary road		
⋯⋯	road tunnel	③	motorway junction
● ●	towns and villages		

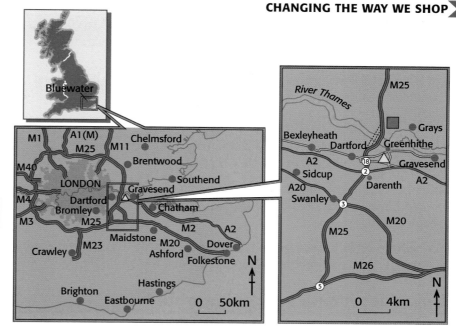

Are there more?

The UK has 11 mega-centres like Bluewater.

They are owned by **developers** – companies who buy land and put up buildings, and then rent them out.

Now the government is worried about their effect on nearby towns, and on traffic. It has not given permission to build more.

▶ *The boating lake at Bluewater.*

Your turn

1 Would *you* enjoy a day out at Bluewater? Give reasons.

2 a Bluewater was built by *developers*. What are developers?

 b Look at the photos and maps for Bluewater. Why did the developers choose this site? Think of at least three reasons.

 c Why didn't they build Bluewater in London?

3 Every new development affects an area. Some people gain, some lose. Look at the maps. How do you think Bluewater will have affected:

 a a small dress shop in Gravesend?

 b shops in central London?

 c the Lakeside shopping centre?

 d a coffee shop at Greenhithe railway station?

 e a small newsagent's in Darenth?

 f traffic on the A2 and M25? Give reasons for your answers.

4 You work for the developers. Make up a leaflet to give local people, to say how Bluewater is helping the area. (Don't forget jobs, and what the site was like before.) Give your leaflet a snappy title.

5 You live in a town near Bluewater: Bexleyheath. The shops there have lost customers to Bluewater. They want you to save them!

 a Think up ways to attract shoppers back to the town.

 b Then prepare a speech to make to the town's Chamber of Commerce, giving your ideas.

In this unit you'll learn how internet shopping works – and explore the pros and cons for different groups of people.

The sky's the limit?

Shops need to be where lots of customers can reach them easily. So why not set up shop in people's homes!

Internet shopping is the latest big change in shopping. It depends on people having computers – just like out-of-town shopping depends on people having transport.

The **sphere of influence** of a shop is the area from which it can draw customers. With the internet, a shop can reach the world!

How does internet shopping work?

The internet is a network of millions of computers around the world, all linked together. The idea was first thought of by an American in 1962. The world's first internet message was sent in 1969, between scientists at two American universities.

Today, you connect your computer to the network using the phone line.

Suppose you want to buy a book from a company called Bookworm in America. This is how it works:

▲ *And we'll have three of those, thank you!*

Key

- ⊙ computers in homes, schools and offices
- ⬤ large computers run by companies called **service providers**. They pass messages around the internet.
- ▬ the route your order could take
- ═ links between computers

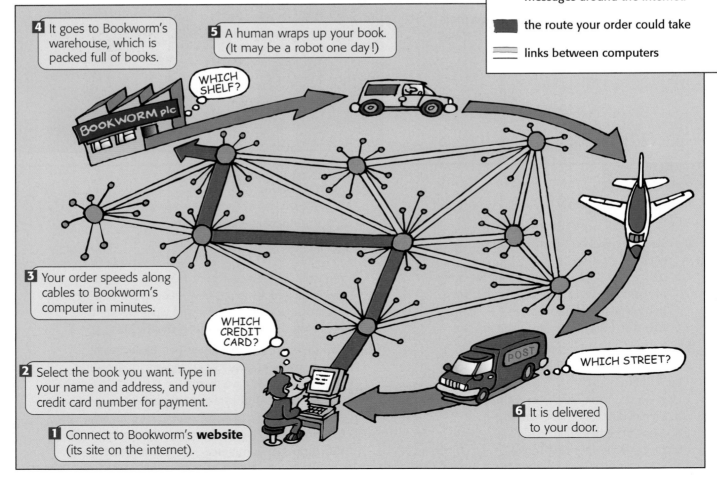

4 It goes to Bookworm's warehouse, which is packed full of books.

5 A human wraps up your book. (It may be a robot one day!)

WHICH SHELF?

BOOKWORM plc

3 Your order speeds along cables to Bookworm's computer in minutes.

WHICH CREDIT CARD?

2 Select the book you want. Type in your name and address, and your credit card number for payment.

1 Connect to Bookworm's **website** (its site on the internet).

WHICH STREET?

6 It is delivered to your door.

What else can you buy?

It's not just books. You can buy almost anything over the internet, from anywhere in the world. Including:

▲ *Delivered to your door.*

Your turn

1 Explain what the *internet* is, in your own words.

2 What would you say is the *main* difference between internet shopping and ordinary shopping, for:
   a the shopper?
   b the company selling the goods?

3 Look at each item in the list below. Would you be happy to buy it over the internet? Give reasons.
   a a computer game
   b designer jeans
   c a week's supply of groceries
   d a new house
   e a packet of crisps

4 You want to set up a new travel agency. Your choice is:

   A   B

   rent a shop in the   create a website and
   middle of the city,   sell tickets and tours
   and do it up nicely   over the internet

   a Which do you think would cost less to run? Why?
   b Which would give you a larger sphere of influence? How big could this sphere of influence be?
   c Which will let you sell tickets more cheaply? Why?

5 Every day, more and more people go internet shopping.

   How do you think this will affect:
   a the local corner shop?
   b a travel agent's in town?
   c an out-of-town shopping centre like Bluewater?
   d air pollution?
   e the number of jobs in shops?
   f companies that deliver parcels?

6 Explain why internet shopping could make life easier for:
   a someone living in a rural area
   b a disabled person
   c a mother with young children
   d a person who works very long hours.

7 Imagine a future where all shopping is over the internet.
   a What effect do you think this would have on:
      i our town centres? ii people's enjoyment of life?
   b Do you think this change would be *sustainable*? (Glossary?) Give your reasons.

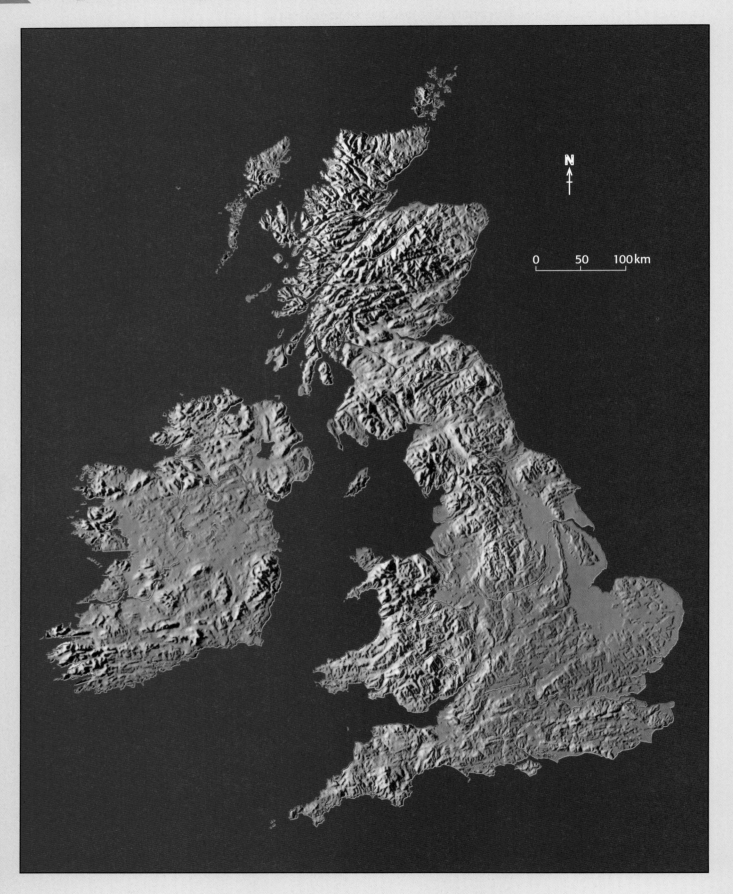

The big picture

This chapter is about Britain – where you live. These are the big ideas behind the chapter:

◆ Britain has been shaped and changed by natural and human processes. This is still going on today.

◆ We think that humans began to settle here about 10 000 years ago, when the ice melted at the end of an Ice Age.

◆ We have now spread all over Britain, farming it, mining it, and building on it.

◆ We have carved it up like a jigsaw, into different regions.

◆ It is a place of contrasts. Some parts are colder and wetter than others. Some are more crowded. Some are more wealthy.

Did you know?
◆ Once upon a time, wild rhino, elephants and lions lived in Britain.

Your goals for this chapter

By the end of this chapter you should be able to answer these questions:

◆ Which countries and nations make up the British Isles?

◆ What are the main physical features of Britain?

◆ What kind of climate do we have in Britain?

◆ Who are the people of Britain descended from?

◆ Which parts of Britain are the most crowded? And least crowded?

◆ What do these terms mean?

urban area   rural area   population density

◆ Which are the UK's ten biggest cities, and where are they?

◆ What kinds of work do people in the UK do?

◆ What do these terms mean?

economic activity   primary sector   secondary sector tertiary sector   services   manufacturing   industry

◆ Which parts of Britain are wealthiest, and which are poorest?

Did you know?
◆ Millions of years ago, Britain had lots of volcanoes.
◆ You can still see volcanic rock in some places.

And then …

When you finish the chapter, come back to this page and see if you have met your goals!

Did you know?
◆ The British Isles used to be joined to the rest of Europe.
◆ But they got cut off by rising seas, and floods, about 8000 years ago.

Your chapter starter

Page 54 shows the islands where you live, and their main rivers.

Can you point out exactly where you live?

What do the squiggly red lines show? And why is one of them thicker?

Where are the highest mountains? And where's the flattest land?

What are the names of the seas around the islands?

Key

 mountainous

 hilly

 quite flat

Your island home

In this unit you'll learn about the forces that shaped the British Isles – and about Britain's main physical features.

All change!

Your island home was not always an island. And not always here!

Once upon a time, the British Isles lay at the equator, as part of a giant continent. When this broke up, they drifted north as part of Europe.

As they drifted, over millions of years, they went through many changes. They became desert. They were frozen in ice. They were drowned by the sea. They had earthquakes and eruptions. They got pushed and squeezed until mountains grew. And then they got cut off from the rest of Europe!

And here are the British Isles today, shaped by all those changes – and still changing.

And finally, our land is also being shaped and changed by humans! We haven't been here that long, but we've made a huge difference.

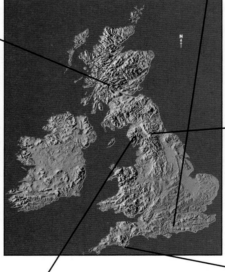

The main cause of those changes was the powerful currents inside the Earth. These drag slabs of the Earth's crust around, causing earthquakes and eruptions, and pushing rock up into mountains.

Rivers, wind, air, rain – all these helped to shape our land, and still do. This river is busy carving out its V-shaped valley.

Did you know?
- The currents inside the Earth are still at work.
- So 100 million years from now, the British Isles will be somewhere else!

Ice also played a big part. In the Ice Ages, glaciers scoured out huge U-shaped valleys in Britain. You can still see them today.

The sea drowned us over and over, dumping sediment that formed new rock. It turned us into islands. And it's still busy shaping the coast.

▲ *You'll find places like this in Britain …*

▲ *… and places like this.*

Your turn

1 This map shows the mountains that formed when rock got squeezed upwards, and some other features of the British Isles.

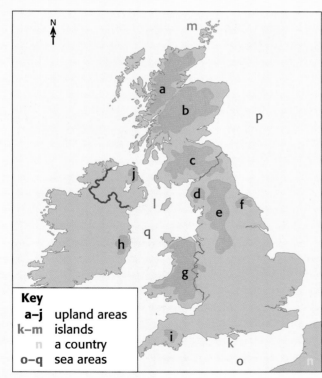

Key
a–j upland areas
k–m islands
n a country
o–q sea areas

Your first task is to name all the places and features marked on the map. Page 127 will help.
Start your answer like this: *a* = _____

2 There are thousands of rivers in Britain, all busy shaping the land. See if you can identify these. (Page 127 will help.)
   A It's the longest river in Britain. It rises in Wales.
   B This one flows by the Houses of Parliament.
   C Stoke-on-Trent sits on this river.
   D Newcastle sits on this one.
   E This one runs along part of the border between England and Scotland.
   F Did Aberdeen get part of its name from this?
   G This one flows to the Wash, on the North Sea.

3 The photos above were taken at A and B on this map.
   a Which photo was taken at which place? Explain your choice.
   b Both places were shaped by nature.
      i Which one also shows signs of being shaped by humans?
      ii What do you think it may have looked like, before humans arrived?
   c Write a paragraph comparing the two places. Say what's similar about them, and what's different.

4 You live on an island. Do you think that's a good thing? Make a list of the advantages of living on an island, and then list the disadvantages.

5 Finally, write a paragraph saying where on the Earth the British Isles is, at present. Include these terms: *equator   ocean   continent   Arctic Circle*

In this unit you'll see how we humans have carved up the British Isles.

Building borders

8000 years ago there were no borders in these islands – because hardly anyone lived here.

But over time, different tribes arrived. They fought over things like land, trade and religion.

Eventually these borders were created between different areas. They still cause problems today!

That's just the start!

As the last map above shows, the British Isles is divided into two **countries**: the United Kingdom (UK) and the Republic of Ireland.

The United Kingdom in turn is made up of different **nations**: England, Scotland, Wales and Northern Ireland. But that's just the start of the jigsaw. For example England is divided into the **regions** on map A below:

These regions are in turn divided into even smaller pieces, as shown on map B.

Dividing it up makes it easier to manage services such as education, and health.

Remember!

the British Isles

the United Kingdom

Great Britain
(or just Britain)

Some facts about the British Isles

Area (square kilometres)	130 400	77 100	20 800	14 200	70 300
Population (millions)	49.2	5.1	2.9	1.7	3.9

Fact box

1801: Ireland becomes part of 'The United Kingdom of Great Britain and Ireland'.

1922: the Republic of Ireland gains independence.

1171: King Henry II of England takes control of Ireland.

1100: England, Scotland, Wales and Ireland are separate countries.

1276: King Edward I of England takes control of Wales.

1536: Henry VIII officially unites England and Wales.

1707: England, Scotland and Wales officially become Great Britain.

Today: England, Scotland, Wales and Northern Ireland are still united as the UK.

Your turn

1 The British Isles is divided like a jigsaw into smaller and smaller pieces.
Walter lives in all these parts of the jigsaw:

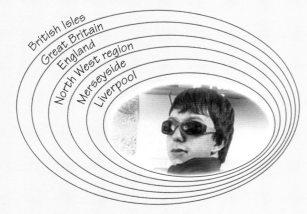

British Isles
Great Britain
England
North West region
Merseyside
Liverpool

Do the same to show where you live.
(But if you live in Liverpool, do it for a person living in Land's End. See the map on page 127.)
You may need to ask your teacher for help.

2 Compare the two maps on page 58.
Name three of the 'jigsaw pieces' within:
  a the Eastern region   **b** the South West
  c the West Midlands   **d** the North West
  e the East Midlands

3 In which region of England is:
  a Oxfordshire? **b** Suffolk? **c** Bristol?

4 a Make your own copy of this table.
(Just sketch the maps roughly.)

	Great Britain	United Kingdom	British Isles
Population (millions)			
Area (____)			

  b Shade in the correct parts of each map.
  c Work out the population and area of the shaded parts, from the table at the top of the page.
  d Now give your table a suitable title.

5 Over the centuries, England fought many battles with Ireland, Scotland and Wales. Much blood was shed. The Fact box above shows just some key dates in this history. (No blood on show !)
Draw a timeline for the dates in the Fact box, from 1100 to today. (There is an example of a timeline in question **2**, page 63.)
You could illustrate your timeline with small maps or flags or other symbols. Give it a suitable title.

What's our climate like?

In this unit you'll learn the difference between weather and climate – and how the climate varies across the UK.

Weather and climate

Weather means the state of the atmosphere. Is it warm? wet? windy? It changes from day to day.

Look at this weather map. With help from the key, you can tell that around A that day:

◆ it was quite cloudy and wet, but there was some sunshine.

◆ the temperature was around 6 °C.

◆ there was a south west wind (it blew *from* the south west).

◆ the wind was quite strong (around 38 miles per hour).

Climate is different from weather. It means what the weather is *usually* like. It is worked out by measuring the weather over many years, and then calculating the average.

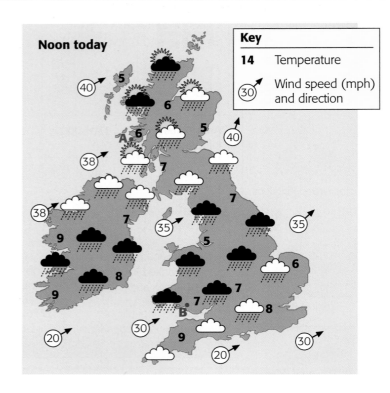

Noon today

Key
14 Temperature
30 Wind speed (mph) and direction

Which parts are warmest? coldest?

Here are two climate maps. They show the *average* temperatures in summer and winter. The wavy lines are **isotherms**. Everywhere along an isotherm has the same average temperature. (*Iso-* means *the same*.)

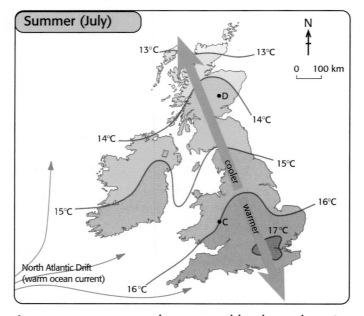

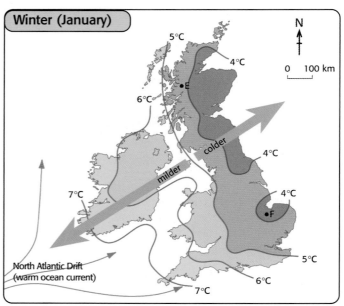

As you can see, some places are colder than others. In general:

◆ It is colder in the north, because it is further from the equator.

◆ It is also colder on high land. Up a mountain the temperature falls.

◆ But in winter, a warm ocean current called the **North Atlantic Drift** warms the west coast. So the east coast is the coldest part in winter.

Which parts are wettest?

On the right is another climate map. It shows the average rainfall in a year, for the British Isles. As you can see, some parts get a lot more rain than others.

Usually the higher parts are wetter. This is why:

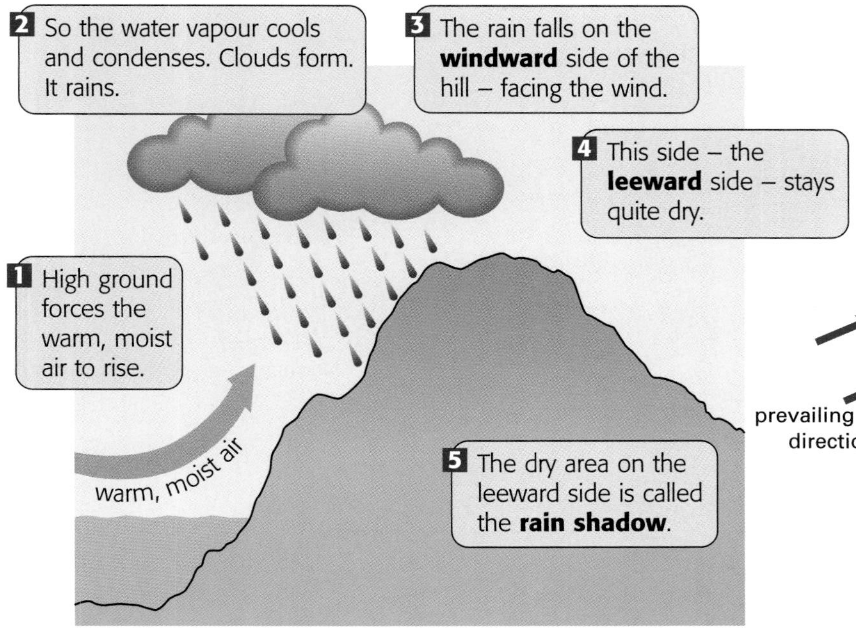

Average annual rainfall

N

2 So the water vapour cools and condenses. Clouds form. It rains.

3 The rain falls on the **windward** side of the hill – facing the wind.

4 This side – the **leeward** side – stays quite dry.

1 High ground forces the warm, moist air to rise.

warm, moist air

5 The dry area on the leeward side is called the **rain shadow**.

prevailing wind direction

Key

average annual rainfall (mm)

mm
2400
1800
1200
800
600

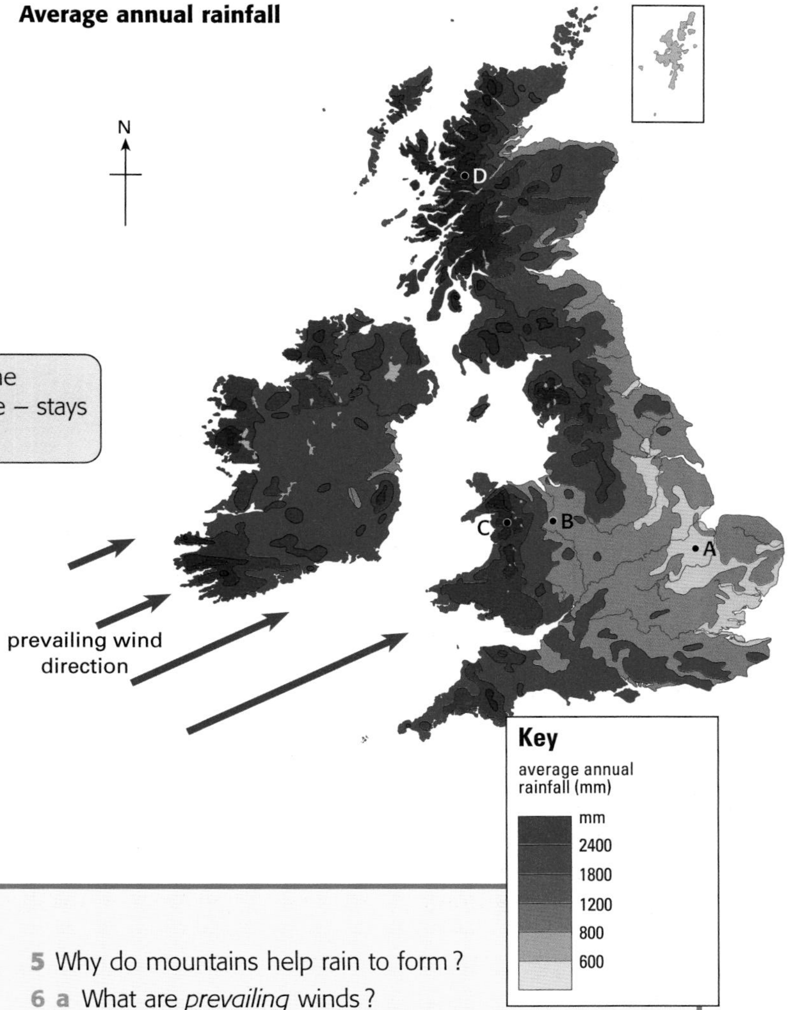

Your turn

1 Look at the TV weather map on page 60.
  Find the place marked B.
  Describe what the weather was like in that area that day, as fully as you can.

2 Look at the first map at the bottom of page 60.
  a What is the temperature at C?
  b Which is the temperature at D?
    15 °C   14 °C   between 14 °C and 15 °C
  c Why is C warmer than D?

3 Now look at the second map.
  a What is the temperature at E?
  b What is the temperature at F?
  c Why is E warmer than F, even though it is further north?

4 Look at the rainfall map above.
  Four places are marked on it: A, B, C and D.
  a Which of them is wettest?
  b Which is driest?
  c One has an average rainfall of 2000 mm a year. Which one?
  d One has an annual rainfall of 500 mm a year. Which one?

5 Why do mountains help rain to form?

6 a What are *prevailing* winds?
  b The prevailing winds in the UK carry lots of moisture. Why? (Think about where they come from. The map on pages 128–129 will help.)

7 a Overall, which side of Great Britain is wettest? See if you can explain why. (Page 54?)
  b Now explain why B gets much less rain than C.

8 And now for a summary of what you've learned.
  On this map the British Isles is divided into four climate zones.
  a Make a larger, simpler, copy of the map.
  b Colour the land in each zone in a different colour.
  c Then add these four labels to their correct zones.

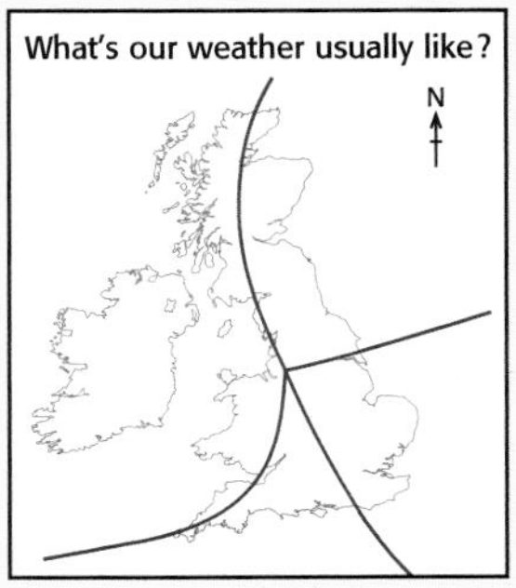

  warm summers, mild winters, not so wet

  mild summers, mild winters, wet

What's our weather usually like?

N

warm summers, cold winters, dry

mild summers, cold winters, not so wet

Who are we?

In this unit you'll find out how Britain has been peopled by immigrants.

The long march

An **immigrant** is a person who moves into a new country to live. 10 000 years ago, nobody was living here. So all British people are descended from immigrants – even the Queen!

People from all over world have moved here, as this drawing shows:

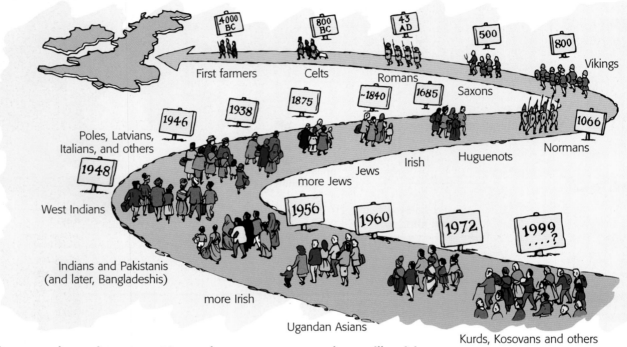

These are the main groups. Many others came too – and are still arriving.

The main arrivals: a summary

Who?	From where?	Start of main wave	Reason
First farmers	Europe	~ 4000 BC	To find a good place to farm.
Celts	central Europe	800 BC	To find land to farm and metals to mine.
Romans	Italy	43 AD	To take control and extend the Roman Empire.
Saxons	Germany	500	First came here to work as paid soldiers. Then took over.
Vikings	Norway	800	First as raiders. Then some settled here.
Normans	France	1066	To take control.
Huguenots	France	1685	To escape persecution (cruel treatment).
Irish	Ireland	~1840	To escape poverty and famine.
Jewish people	Eastern Europe	1875	To escape persecution.
More Jewish people	All over Europe	1938	To escape persecution.
Poles, Latvians, Italians and others	From Europe	1946	The British government invited them here to work. (We had a shortage of workers after World War II.)
West Indians	The Caribbean	1948	To find work.
Indians and Pakistanis (and later, Bangladeshis)*	India and Pakistan	1956	Same.
Lots more Irish	Ireland	1960	Same.
Ugandan Asians	Uganda	1972	Thrown out of Uganda by the dictator Idi Amin.
Kurds, Kosovans and others	Kurdistan, Kosovo and other war-torn places	1999–???	Driven from their country by war.

* East Pakistan became Bangladesh in 1971.

All mixed up

So we carry the genes of past immigrants in our body cells. Like this…

Descended from Turval, a Celtic story teller. Sadly he died from teeth problems.

Descended from an Indian princess called Sita, who wrote wonderful poetry.

Descended from Heloise, a Huguenot silk weaver who married a London baker.

Descended from Vladinski, a Russian Jew who eloped with an Irish cook.

Descended from a Viking boat builder who fell in love with a girl from Northumberland.

Descended from Claudius, a Roman commander who lived in York.

Who do you think you are descended from?

Your turn

1 What is an *immigrant*?

2 This shows the start of a **time line** for the main groups of immigrants since the year 1 AD.

Romans
(43 AD)

Saxons
(500 AD)

Start of AD   500   1000   1500   2000   Year (AD)

Now draw your own time line for them.
a First draw a line 21 cm long. Divide and label it, with 1 cm for each century.
b Draw a line for the Romans at 43 AD. Label it.
c Repeat for the other groups in the table.
   After 1900 it gets crowded – so take care. (It will help if you make your lines different lengths.)

3 Now look at your time line.
a When was the biggest gap between new arrivals?
b In which century did most new groups arrive?

4 Look at these different terms:
   A refugee   **B** invader   **C** migrant
   D emigrant   **E** asylum seeker **F** settler
a First, write down what each term means. (Glossary.)
b Then choose what you think is the best term for each person in the photos on the right.

5 a Why did the first immigrants want to come here?
  b What do you think attracts new immigrants today? Think of as many factors as you can.

▲ William the Conqueror, the Norman who took control of England by force in 1066.

▲ Chiyo in a Red Cross camp after her home was destroyed by an earthquake.

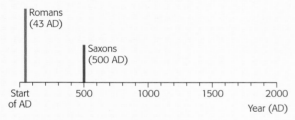

▲ Philip, tortured by the army in his own country, has asked permission to stay here.

▲ Joy arriving from Jamaica in 1956. She wants to find a job.

Where do we live?

In this unit you'll see how we humans have shaped the country, through where we chose to live !

Population density

About 63 million people live in the British Isles. 59 million of us live in the UK. So are we all spread out evenly ? The answer of course is No !

The **population density** of a place is the average number of people per square kilometre.

The map below shows how population density changes around the British Isles. The deep green regions are the least crowded. The deep red regions are the most crowded. As you can see, the population density varies a lot.

The UK's 10 largest cities

	Name	Population (millions)
1	London	7.17
2	Birmingham	0.98
3	Leeds	0.72
4	Glasgow	0.58
5	Sheffield	0.51
6	Bradford	0.47
7	Edinburgh	0.45
8	Liverpool	0.44
9	Manchester	0.39
10	Bristol	0.38

Did you know?
Of all the countries in the world, the UK ranks:
• 18th for size of population
• 45th for population density.

Did you know?
• London is the 26th largest city in the world.
• The largest one is Tokyo in Japan (population 26.8 million).

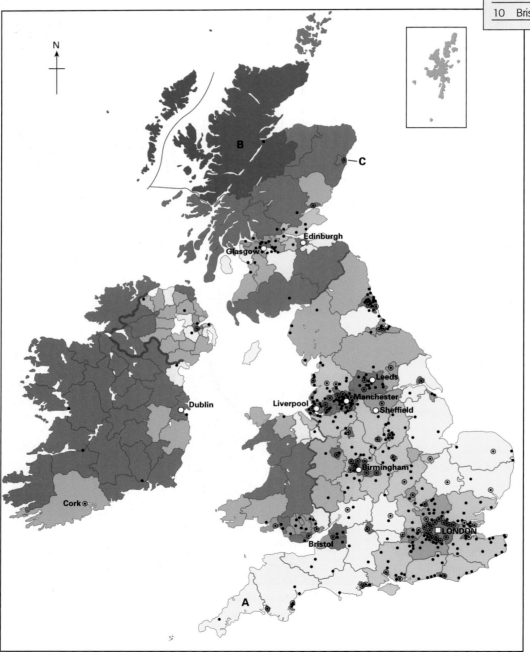

Key

people per square kilometre

- over 1000
- 500–1000
- 250–500
- 100–250
- 50–100
- 10–50
- under 10

Major cities and towns

number of people

- □ over 1 000 000
- ○ 400 000–1 000 000
- ◉ 100 000–400 000
- • 25 000–100 000

▲ *Some places in the UK are quite empty, while some ...*

▲ *... are very crowded. What's your place like?*

Your turn

1 Compare the two photos above.
  a Which place has the higher population density?
  b Which place is: **i** an urban area? **ii** a rural area? (Glossary?)

2 Look at the map on page 64. Some areas have been labelled with letters.
  a **i** What is the population density for area A? Give your answer in persons per square kilometre.
    ii Do you think *every* part of area A has the same number of people per sq km? Explain.
  b **i** What is the population density for area B?
    ii See if you can explain why it's so low. (Page 54?)
  c Area C has a much higher population density than the area around it. Can you suggest a reason? (Page 68 has a clue.)
  d **i** Overall, where is the largest area of highest population density, in the British Isles?
    ii Suggest a reason why so many people live here. (Check out page 67?)

3 The *average* population density for the UK is 242 people per sq km.
  Copy this table and see if you can fill in the names of the four nations (England, Wales, Northern Ireland, Scotland) in the correct places in the first column. The map on page 64 will help.

Nation	Average pop. density (persons/sq km)
	377
	120
	66
	139

4 Look at the map again. The main cities and towns are marked in. Can you see any link between the number of cities and towns in a region, and its population density? Explain.

5 Now look at this pie chart for the United Kingdom.

Where the UK population lives

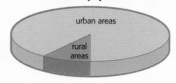

Is this statement true or false?
  a Most people in the UK live in the countryside.
  b Less than half of us live in towns and cities.
  c About $\frac{1}{10}$ of the UK population lives in rural areas.

6 Next look at the list of UK top 10 cities on page 64.
  a Which two of the cities are in Scotland?
  b Where are the other eight?
  c Which is the largest city of all? How many times larger is it than: **i** Birmingham? **ii** Bristol?

7 Towns and cities can grow and spread until they join up, giving large built-up areas called **conurbations**. From the map on page 64, name 5 cities in *England* which are probably part of conurbations.

8 And finally, to round off this unit, write a report called *The pattern of population density around the UK*. Make it 100 – 150 words. Say clearly where the most crowded and least crowded regions are, and add other interesting details.

What kind of work do we do?

In this unit you'll find out what kinds of work people in the UK do for a living.

Different kinds of work

Economic activity is any work people get paid for.
(So homework does not count!)
You can divide it into four types or **sectors**:

Primary
Gathering materials from the Earth. For example mining for coal, or growing wheat, or fishing.

Secondary or **manufacturing**
You turn materials into things to sell. For example metal into car bodies or fish into fish nuggets.

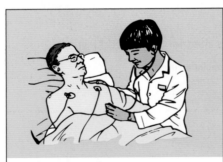

Tertiary or **service**
You provide a service for people. Like teach them, or look after them when they're ill, or drive a taxi.

Quaternary
Hi-tech research. For example to develop a new medicine, or more advanced mobile phones.

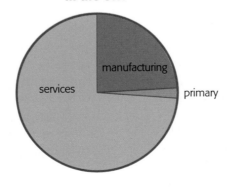

▲ On the way to work, on a dark morning. (The truck drivers are working already.)

At work in the UK

Altogether, about 26 million people in the UK work for a living.

As this pie chart shows, most of them provide services.

The number in the quaternary sector is too small to show up!

What kind of work do we do, in the UK?

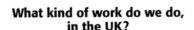

services — manufacturing — primary

What is an industry?

Industry is just a general word for a branch of economic activity.
The car industry is made up of all the companies who make cars.

Economic activity in the UK

This map shows some of the UK's economic activity. Note that:

◆ farming goes on all around the UK. But there is only a little in the very hilly areas, where the farms are far apart. (Look back at the map on page 54.)

◆ lots of people in the UK earn a living from tourism.

◆ most industry is found around large towns and cities. It's one reason why they grew!

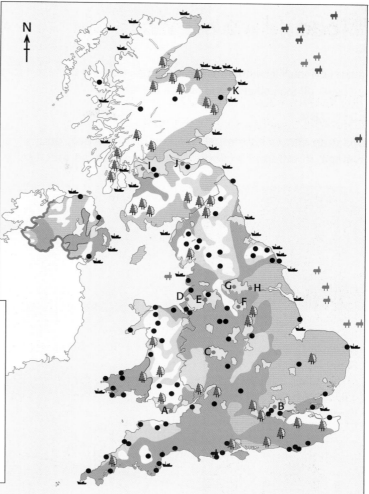

Key

mostly hill farms (sheep)	
mostly livestock farms (animals for meat)	
mostly dairy farms (cattle for milk)	
mostly arable farms (crops)	

🌲 forestry

🛥 fishing port

● main tourism sites

major industrial area

⊥ gas field

⊤ oil field

〜 international border

〜 national border

Your turn

1 What is *economic activity*?

2 Does this count as economic activity? Give a reason.
   a going to school   b doing a paper round
   c babysitting   d tidying your room

3 a Make a table with headings like this:

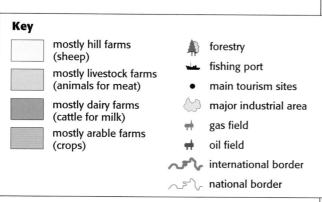

Primary	Secondary	Tertiary	Quaternary

   b Now write these jobs in the correct columns in your table:

   nurse   postman   boat builder
   oil rig worker   actor   florist
   football star   fireman   farmer
   copper miner   architect   policeman
   bank manager   truck driver   bee keeper
   gene researcher clergyman   inventor of robots

   c See if you can add *at least* ten other jobs to your table. Try for some for each sector. (Think about workers you see on TV, or on the way to school.)

4 Copy and complete, using words from the list below. (The pie chart on page 66 will help.)

   In the UK most people earn a living by providing _____. The _____ sector employs about _____ times as many people as _____ does, and about _____ times as many as the _____ _____.

   sector, three, primary, tertiary, manufacturing, services, forty

5 Look at Scotland on the map above. Give:
   a three primary activities off the coast
   b two primary activities on land

6 The map shows where tourism is important. Give six jobs connected with tourism. (Hint: tourists have to eat and sleep and travel.)

7 The map shows the main industrial areas, where you'll find factories. Compare these with the map of population density on page 64. What do you notice?

8 The red dots on the map above show 11 cities important for industry. (9 are in the 'top 10' list on page 64.) Name them. Start like this: A = _____ .

Richer? Poorer?

In this unit you'll learn that some parts of Great Britain
are better off than others – and explore the reasons.

Fair pay?

This map shows how much workers earn a week, on
average, in different regions. Why does it vary so much?

Key
Income, 2000
average weekly earnings

	over £475
	£425–£475
	£400–£425
	£375–£400
	£350–£375
	under £350
	no data

Earnings are high here
because of the oil industry.
The oil fields are in the
North Sea.

100 years ago this area
was wealthy – thanks to
shipbuilding and other
heavy industries. But most
of them died away and the
area grew poor. Now it is
trying hard to recover.

This area was once
wealthier because of coal.
Now the mines are closed.
(It's the same in Wales and
other coal areas.)

This area has hardly any
industry. But it has beautiful
countryside and depends
heavily on tourists.

Lots of new hi-tech
companies are setting up
in this area too.

This area never had many
factories. The land is not so
good for farming. There
used to be tin mines but
they have closed.

Earnings are high in this
area because it has lots of
hi-tech companies (making
computers, software,
mobile phones and so on).

London is the capital city,
and a major centre of
government, business, and
tourism. Companies have
head offices here. There
are many highly paid jobs.

This has some of the UK's
best farmland. It grows
large amounts of crops.

▲ You can tell a lot about how wealthy or poor an area is, just by looking.

Your turn

1 This list gives weekly earnings for five people. Work out their *average* weekly earning. (Hint: add up and divide by 5.)

Brian	£400
Liz	£50
Anna	£500
Joe	£250
Richard	£1000

2 Look at the map on page 68.
   a What's the average weekly earning at A?
   b Does everyone in area A earn this much? Explain.
   c What's the average weekly earning at B?
   d Give reasons for the big difference in the figures for A and B.

3 Look at C on the map. Earnings in this area are higher than in the other areas around it. See if you can come up with a reason. (The map on page 67 may help.)

4 **a** Overall, where in Britain do people earn most?
   b Where do they earn least?
   Use terms like these in your answers: *south west, Wales, England, north of* and so on.

5 So what helps to make an area wealthy?
   Show your answer as a spider map, like this one:

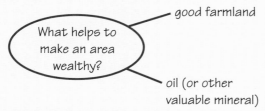

Page 68 will give you clues.

6 Now look at photos A and B at the top of the page.
   a Compare the two places. Which one seems to be poorer? What is your evidence?
   b What clues can you find that this place is poorer than it used to be?
   c What might have caused this change?

7 The government tries to help poorer areas. For example by:
   ◆ giving companies grants to set up new factories
   ◆ giving grants to improve roads and tourist facilities.
   This flow chart shows how a new factory can help a poorer area.

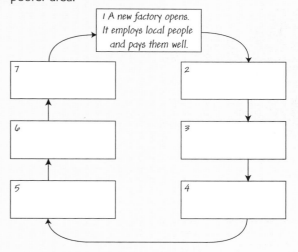

Make a much larger copy. (Use a whole page). Then write these in the correct boxes:

So the local people have more money to spend.

So the shops get better, and other services (like restaurants and sports centres) open.

So they buy more clothes and shoes and other goods.

... so more companies think about moving there.

So the area becomes more attractive to live and work in ...

So the local shops make more money.

8 Now do your own flow chart, to show how a new tourist attraction (for example a new nature park, or an exciting new museum) could help a poor area.

The big picture

There are millions of rivers on the Earth, and about 5000 in the UK ! This chapter is all about rivers. These are the big ideas behind the chapter:

◆ A river is just rainwater flowing to the sea.

◆ On the way it cuts and shapes the land, like a sculptor.

◆ It does this by picking up bits of rock and soil from one place, and carrying them to another.

◆ The result is special landforms along the river.

◆ The river is helped in its work by weathering, which breaks rock into bits that the river can carry away.

Your goals for this chapter

By the end of this chapter you should be able to answer these questions:

◆ What is the water cycle?

◆ How does the rainfall from the water cycle feed a river?

◆ What do these river terms mean?

source   mouth   channel   bed   banks   tributary   confluence
drainage basin   watershed   flood plain

◆ What is weathering, and how does it happen?

◆ How do rivers shape the land? And how does weathering help?

◆ How do these get formed?

a V-shaped valley   a waterfall   a meander   an oxbow lake

And then …

When you finish the chapter, come back to this page and see if you have met your goals!

Did you know?
◆ The River Nile, in Africa, is the world's longest river (6695 km).
◆ It's 20 times longer than the longest British river, the Severn.

Did you know?
◆ The River Amazon is the world's largest river – it carries the most water.
◆ Its mouth is over 200 km wide.

Did you know?
◆ Water is the most common substance on the Earth.
◆ But less than 1% of it is in rivers.
◆ 97% is in the oceans – and that's salty!

Did you know?
◆ Every year the world's rivers carry about 10 billion tonnes of material to the sea.

Your chapter starter

Look at the photo on page 70.

What's going on here? Do you think it's dangerous?

Where did the water come from? And where is it going to?

Why is it swirling and foaming?

Do you think the river will look like this all the way along? Explain.

No, I did NOT get my socks wet.

The water cycle

In this unit you'll learn about the water cycle, and how the rainfall reaches a river.

What is the water cycle?

Water sloshing around in the ocean this week may fall on you next week – as rain. It's the **water cycle** at work. Follow the numbers to see how water cycles between the ocean, the air and the land:

4 ... **precipitation**. The water drops fall as rain (or hail or sleet or snow). You need a raincoat.

3 The clouds get carried along by the wind. The droplets inside them grow into larger drops, leading to ...

2 The air rises. High up, where it's cooler, the water vapour **condenses** into tiny water droplets. These form clouds.

5 Some water runs along the ground, and some soaks through it, heading for streams and rivers.

1 The sun warms oceans, lakes and seas, turning water into water vapour, a gas. This is called **evaporation**.

6 The river carries the water back to the ocean. The cycle is complete. And then it starts all over again ...

The water cycle and us

Without the water cycle we'd be in big trouble. We depend on rivers for water for homes and factories, and for spraying crops. And rivers depend on rain!

Every year, the UK 'borrows' about 17 thousand billion litres of water from the water cycle. It is pumped from rivers and lakes and underground rocks, where rain has trickled down. It is cleaned up and used in homes and factories. And then our dirty water goes down the plug hole, gets cleaned up at a treatment plant, and is poured back into the river.

▲ *Borrowing from the water cycle.*

How the rainfall reaches the river

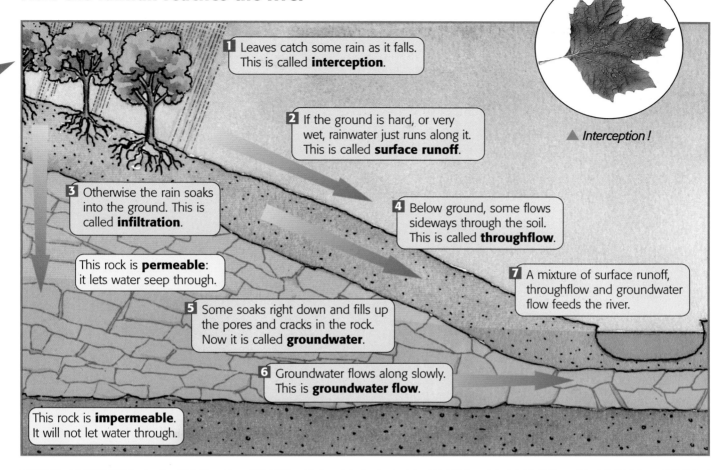

1 Leaves catch some rain as it falls. This is called **interception**.

2 If the ground is hard, or very wet, rainwater just runs along it. This is called **surface runoff**.

3 Otherwise the rain soaks into the ground. This is called **infiltration**.

4 Below ground, some flows sideways through the soil. This is called **throughflow**.

This rock is **permeable**: it lets water seep through.

7 A mixture of surface runoff, throughflow and groundwater flow feeds the river.

5 Some soaks right down and fills up the pores and cracks in the rock. Now it is called **groundwater**.

6 Groundwater flows along slowly. This is **groundwater flow**.

This rock is **impermeable**. It will not let water through.

▲ *Interception !*

Your turn

1 a Make a larger copy of this flow chart for the water cycle. (At least twice as large.)

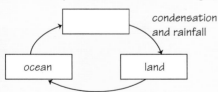

condensation and rainfall

ocean

land

b Then add these labels in the correct places:
atmosphere   rivers flow over land   evaporation

2 A – H below are definitions.
a You have to find the matching words, in the text !
b Then write out the words and their definitions.

   A lets water pass through
   B this water is held in rock, underground
   C when water soaks down through the ground (*i*....)
   D a longer name for rainfall
   E the process that turns water into a gas (*e*....)
   F the trapping of rain by leaves
   G the process that turns water vapour into water
   H does not let water pass through

3

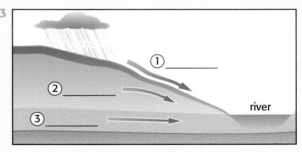

① _____
② _____
③ _____
river

Draw a diagram like the one above, to show how rainwater reaches a river. Add the missing labels and a title.

4 Give reasons to explain why:
   a rain does not sink down to the centre of the Earth
   b a river can keep flowing even in very dry weather
   c the river level falls, when there's a drought
   d a river can fill up very fast in very wet weather

5 Suddenly the water cycle stops working. No more evaporation from the ocean ! No more rain !
Write a radio report about the effect this will have on us. Make it dramatic – and not more than 250 words.

A river on its journey

In this unit you'll learn about the different parts of a river – and then take a look at the River Coquet!

The parts of a river

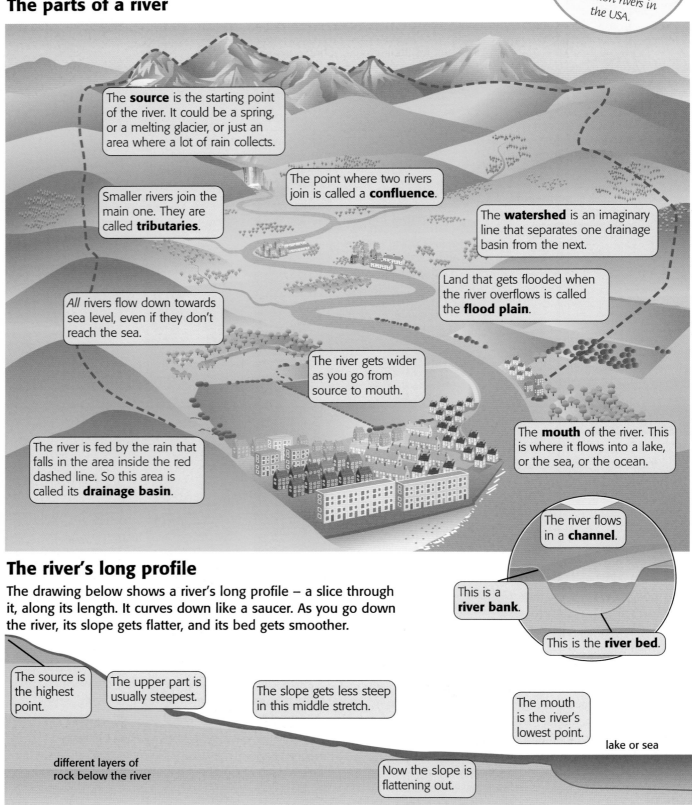

The **source** is the starting point of the river. It could be a spring, or a melting glacier, or just an area where a lot of rain collects.

The point where two rivers join is called a **confluence**.

Smaller rivers join the main one. They are called **tributaries**.

The **watershed** is an imaginary line that separates one drainage basin from the next.

All rivers flow down towards sea level, even if they don't reach the sea.

Land that gets flooded when the river overflows is called the **flood plain**.

The river gets wider as you go from source to mouth.

The river is fed by the rain that falls in the area inside the red dashed line. So this area is called its **drainage basin**.

The **mouth** of the river. This is where it flows into a lake, or the sea, or the ocean.

The river flows in a **channel**.

This is a **river bank**.

This is the **river bed**.

The river's long profile

The drawing below shows a river's long profile – a slice through it, along its length. It curves down like a saucer. As you go down the river, its slope gets flatter, and its bed gets smoother.

The source is the highest point.

The upper part is usually steepest.

The slope gets less steep in this middle stretch.

The mouth is the river's lowest point.

lake or sea

different layers of rock below the river

Now the slope is flattening out.

Your turn

The River Coquet and its drainage basin

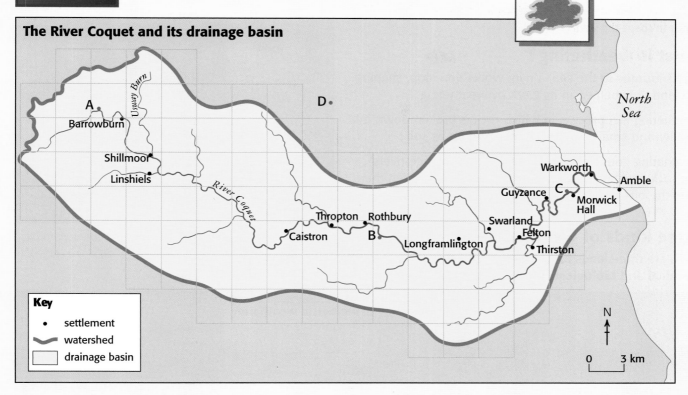

Key
- • settlement
- ⌇ watershed
- ▢ drainage basin

0   3 km

N ↑

1 This is a map of the River Coquet. (You say *Cockette*.) It's in Northumberland.
  a Name the village nearest the source of the river.
  b How many tributaries join the river?
  c Name the settlement nearest the confluence of the Coquet and Usway Burn.
  d What sea does the Coquet flow into?
  e A, B and C mark three fields by the river. Which one:
    i is highest above sea level? ii is lowest?

2 a What is a *drainage basin*?
  b You can work out the area of the river's drainage basin roughly, by counting squares like this:

  Full = 1.   At least   Less than
               half full = 1.   half full = 0.

    i Count the yellow squares as shown.
    ii Each square represents 9 square kilometres. What is the area of the Coquet's drainage basin?

3 How long is the Coquet? Use the scale.
  a 55 km   b 80 km   c 110 km

4 Where is the river's long profile likely to be steeper?
  a between Barrowburn and Shillmoor
  b between Guyzance and Morwick Hall
  Explain your answer.

5 Rain falls at D on the map above. Will it end up in the Coquet? If not, where will it go?

6

This photo was taken at the mouth of the river. (The OS map on page 23 also shows this area.)

  a In which direction was the photographer facing?
  b Name the village on the left.
  c This village used to be a Roman settlement. Suggest reasons why the Romans chose this site.
  d What clues can you find from the photo, that this place is now: i a fishing port? ii a holiday resort?

7 Draw a spider map to show all the ways we use rivers – for water, work, and leisure. Make it look fun!

Weathering – the river's helper

In this unit you'll learn what weathering is, and how it helps a river to shape the land.

What is weathering?

On its journey to the sea, a river works non-stop, shaping the land. It is helped in its work by weathering.

Weathering is a process in which rock is broken down into smaller and smaller pieces. It may end up as soil!

Weathering goes on everywhere (not just beside rivers). The rock gets broken down where it sits. A river can then carry the bits away.

▲ Rock breaks down into bits, just like old cars rust to bits.

Three kinds of weathering

There are three kinds of weathering: **physical**, **chemical** and **biological**. They can all go on together.

In **biological weathering** roots grow into cracks and widen them.

In **physical weathering** the rock is broken up by ice, or heat and cold. Like this:

1 Water trickles into cracks. It freezes in icy weather. It expands as it freezes – so the cracks get wider and wider.

2 Some places are very hot in the day and cold at night. The rock expands in the heat, and contracts again when it cools. Over time this breaks it up.

In **chemical weathering** rock reacts with air and water. Like this:

1 Water combines with some minerals in rock and turns them into clay.

2 Carbon dioxide from the air dissolves in rain to form **carbonic acid**. This attacks rock, giving compounds that dissolve.

3 Oxygen from the air reacts with some things in rock. For example it 'rusts' any iron.

See how weathering has already broken some of this rock down into soil.

How fast will the rock break down?

That depends on two things:

◆ the type of rock. Some types weather faster than others.

◆ the climate. For example chemical weathering is much faster in a hot damp climate than in a cold dry one.

From rock to soil

This shows how weathering turns rock into soil:

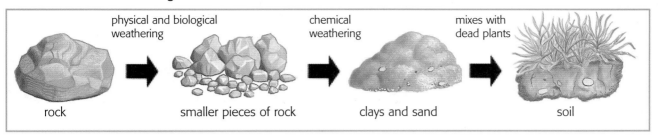

physical and biological weathering → chemical weathering → mixes with dead plants

rock → smaller pieces of rock → clays and sand → soil

In a hot damp climate, a thick layer of soil can form from bare rock in a few hundred years.

Weathering around a river

This shows the ground around a river. Once it was all just rock. Look how the rock has been weathered giving bits the river can carry away.

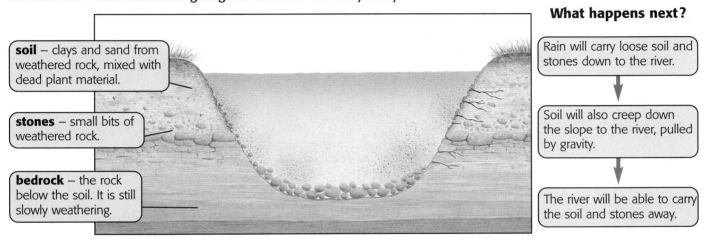

soil – clays and sand from weathered rock, mixed with dead plant material.

stones – small bits of weathered rock.

bedrock – the rock below the soil. It is still slowly weathering.

What happens next?

Rain will carry loose soil and stones down to the river.

Soil will also creep down the slope to the river, pulled by gravity.

The river will be able to carry the soil and stones away.

Your turn

1 Copy and complete, using words from the list below.
_____ is the process that breaks rocks down. In _____ and _____ weathering, the rock just gets broken into _____. But in _____weathering it _____ with air and _____ and is changed into sand and _____.

*reacts physical clays chemical weathering
biological bedrock water pieces organic*

2 Look at the photo on the right.
  a i Under the grass is soil. Where did it come from?
    ii Name the overall process that produced it.
  b If you dig down through the soil, what will you find?
  c The rock under the soil is being weathered, even though it is below ground. Try to explain why.

3 Now explain in your own words how weathering is helping this river to shape the land.

4 Some river water is very brown. Why?

Rivers at work

In this unit you'll learn how rivers shape the land, by picking up, carrying and dropping material.

What work does a river do?

A river never sleeps. It works non-stop, day and night, cutting and shaping and smoothing the land.

Rivers do their work in three stages:

1 they pick up or **erode** material from one place

2 they carry or **transport** it to another place

3 then they drop or **deposit** it.

Now we will look at each of these in more detail.

▲ Hard at work …

1 Erosion

This shows the different ways erosion takes place:

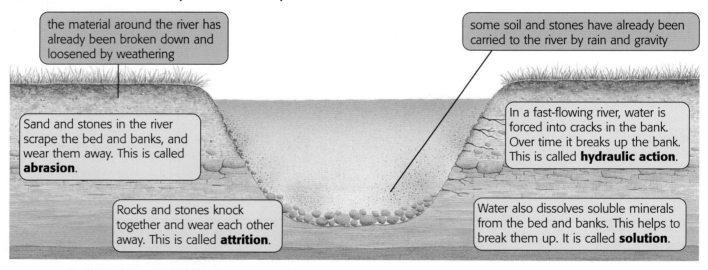

the material around the river has already been broken down and loosened by weathering

some soil and stones have already been carried to the river by rain and gravity

Sand and stones in the river scrape the bed and banks, and wear them away. This is called **abrasion**.

In a fast-flowing river, water is forced into cracks in the bank. Over time it breaks up the bank. This is called **hydraulic action**.

Rocks and stones knock together and wear each other away. This is called **attrition**.

Water also dissolves soluble minerals from the bed and banks. This helps to break them up. It is called **solution**.

The faster it flows, and the more water it has, the faster the river erodes.

2 Transport

The material the river carries is called its **load**.

Heavier material is carried along the bottom. It is called the **bedload**.

Dissolved material is carried along as a solution. You cannot see it.

Sand grains and small stones just bounce along.

Larger stones and rocks get rolled along.

Small particles of rock and soil are carried along as a **suspension**. They make the water look cloudy or muddy.

The faster it flows, and the more water it has, the larger the load the river can carry.

3 Deposition

When it reaches flatter land, the river slows down. It no longer has the energy to carry its load, so it deposits it – just like you put things down when you are tired. The deposited material is called **sediment**.

> But dissolved material stays in the water and is carried out into the lake or sea.

> As the river slows down, it deposits the largest stones and pebbles first, then smaller ones, and finally, the smallest particles.

The slower it flows, the more material the river deposits.

Where does all this happen?

> As the slope flattens the river loses energy – so deposition takes over.

> In this middle part, some material is eroded and some deposited.

> It deposits most of its load in the flat flood plain, and the rest where it enters the sea.

> Erosion is the main job in the upper part of the river, where the bed is steepest and roughest.

Your turn

1   **A** material is carried away   **B** erosion
      material is picked up   deposition
      material is dropped   transport

   a List A shows the jobs that go on in a river. Write them in the correct order.
   b Beside each, write the correct term from B.

2 Now look at the photo on page 78.
   a What work do you think the river is doing here? Say why you think so.
   b What part is being played in this work by:
      i the water itself?   ii stones in the river?
   Give the correct name for each process you mention.

3 a Look at this photo. What job is the river doing at X?
   b Do you think the river is flowing quickly, or slowly, in this stretch? Explain why you think so.
   c Is this area in the flood plain? Explain your answer.

4 During a heavy flood a river can transport trees and large boulders. Explain why.

5 Now look again at the photo on page 78. It was taken in March after a lot of heavy rain.
   a In what ways might the river be different at the end of a very dry summer? Give your reasons.
   b How might this affect the work the river does?

Landforms created by the river

In this unit you'll learn about the landforms a river creates (shown below), by eroding and depositing material.

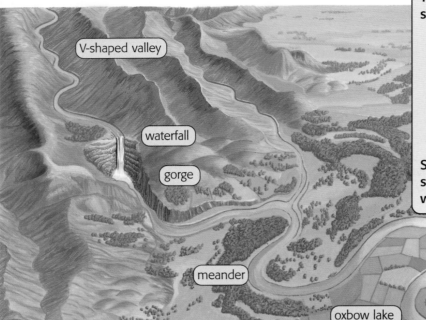

V-shaped valley

waterfall

gorge

meander

oxbow lake

A V-shaped valley

The river cuts down through the land like a saw. This is called **downward erosion**.

Soil and stones then get carried down the slopes by rain and gravity – so the V grows wider and wider.

A waterfall

The water tumbles over a ledge of hard rock.

A waterfall is a sign that there are layers of different rock under the river.

The rock in the top layer does not erode easily. That's why the waterfall forms.

How a waterfall develops

hard rock

soft rock

ledge undercut

plunge pool

1 The soft rock is easy to erode, but the hard rock is not. So, as the years go by, a ledge develops.

2 The water rushes over the ledge and erodes the soft rock, forming a **plunge pool**.

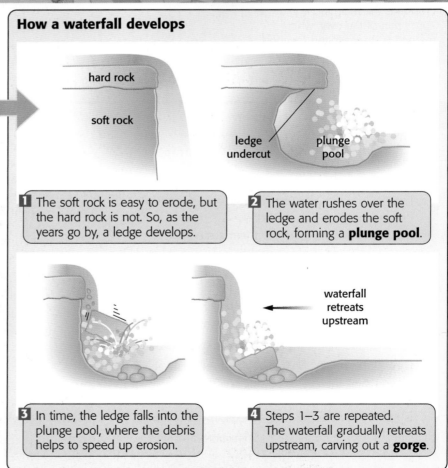

waterfall retreats upstream

3 In time, the ledge falls into the plunge pool, where the debris helps to speed up erosion.

4 Steps 1–3 are repeated. The waterfall gradually retreats upstream, carving out a **gorge**.

How a meander develops

A meander starts as a slight bend. Look how it develops:

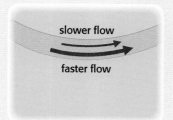
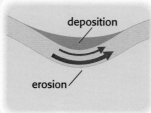
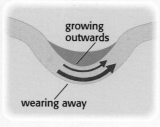
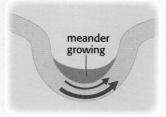

1 Water flows faster on the outer curve of the bend, and slower on the inner curve. So …

2 … the outer bank gets eroded, but material is deposited at the inner bank. Over time …

3 … as the outer bank wears away, and the inner one grows, a meander forms.

4 As the process continues, the meander grows more 'loopy'.

How an oxbow lake develops

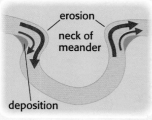
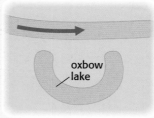
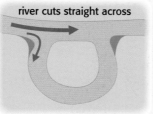
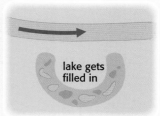

1 An oxbow lake starts as a big meander like this. Thanks to erosion and deposition …

2 … the neck grows narrower and narrower. And eventually the river just takes a shortcut.

3 Soon the loop is sealed off altogether. It turns into an oxbow lake.

4 In time the lake will get covered with weeds, and fill with soil, and disappear.

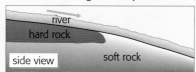

1 Make a table like this one and complete it for all the river landforms shown on these two pages.

Landform	Created by …
V-shaped valley	erosion

2 What is a gorge? (Try the glossary.)

3 A river is flowing over layers of rock, like this:

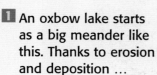

a Which will erode faster, the hard rock or the soft rock?

b Draw diagrams to show how a waterfall will eventually develop.

c Then show how a gorge will form.

4 Look at the scene above.

a What is happening at A? Why?

b What is happening at B? Why?

c Draw a sketch to show how the river might look 500 years from now.

Coping with floods

The big picture

This chapter is all about floods, and how we cope with them. These are the big ideas behind the chapter:

◆ There have always been floods. They are a natural hazard. But we humans are making them worse.

◆ We respond to floods in the short term by helping the flood victims.

◆ We respond to floods in the longer term by trying to prevent them.

◆ There are several ways to prevent them – but none are perfect, and some may do more harm than good.

◆ Helping victims and preventing floods can cost a lot of money, which poorer countries may not be able to afford.

Your goals for this chapter

By the end of this chapter you should be able to answer these questions:

◆ What do these terms mean?

flooding   flood plain   embankment   infrastructure
emergency services   short-term response   long-term response
flood control   silt   delta

◆ What causes floods?

◆ Which *natural* factors increase the risk of floods?

◆ In what ways have we humans increased the risk of floods?

◆ Why does Bangladesh suffer worse flooding than the UK?

◆ How do we cope with floods in the UK – and is it the same in Bangladesh?

◆ Why can wealthier countries cope better with floods (and other natural hazards) than poorer countries?

◆ How do we try to stop places flooding, and which is the best way?

And then ...

When you finish the chapter, come back to this page and see if you have met your goals!

Did you know?
◆ In the UK, about 1 in 12 of us lives in an area at risk of flooding. (What about you?)

Did you know?
◆ The world's worst river for flood deaths is the Yellow River in China.
◆ In 1887 its floods drowned 900 000 people.
◆ Millions more died later from hunger and disease.

Did you know?
◆ Climate change could cause a ten-fold rise in flooding in the UK, this century.

Your chapter starter

Look at the photo on page 82. What's going on here?

How do you think the people feel about it?

What kinds of problems do you think it's causing? (Look closely, for clues!)

Do you think it's anyone's fault?

What do you think will happen to all the water? And when?

There's never a boat when you need one.

Flood alert!

In this unit you will learn what floods are, what causes them, what damage they do – and how we humans can make them worse.

What are floods?

Floods occur when a river gets more water than its channel can hold. So water flows over the banks and onto the flood plain.

What causes them?

Floods are usually caused by heavy rain – but sometimes by ice or snow melting.

A burst of very heavy rain can cause a sudden **flash flood**. People get no warning so they may get trapped, and drown.

This diagram explains how a flood happens.

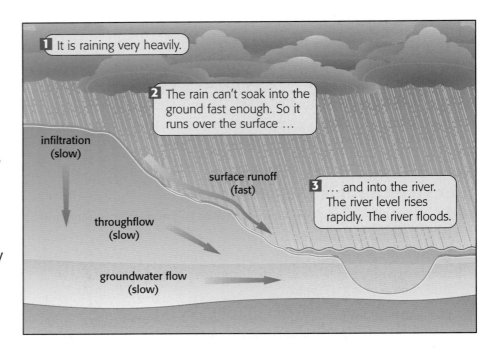

1 It is raining very heavily.

2 The rain can't soak into the ground fast enough. So it runs over the surface …

3 … and into the river. The river level rises rapidly. The river floods.

infiltration (slow)

surface runoff (fast)

throughflow (slow)

groundwater flow (slow)

Factors that increase the risk of flooding

Anything that stops rain soaking into the ground, in the river's drainage basin, will increase the risk of flooding. Here are some examples.

Impermeable rock
There may be impermeable rock such as granite under the soil. So the rain can't soak through.

Hard dry soil
When soil is baked hard by dry weather, rain can't soak through it easily. It will run over it instead.

Very wet soil
If the soil is already saturated, no more rain can soak through. (In fact wet clay swells and seals out water!)

Steep slopes
Rain will run down a steep slope quickly – before it has a chance to soak through the ground.

Cutting down trees
Leaves intercept rain. Roots take in water. So if you cut down lots of trees you get more floods.

Building in the drainage basin
Rain cannot infiltrate streets and pavements. The more building there is, the greater the risk of floods.

The damage floods do

See what can happen when a river floods.

> You may be swept away and drowned. (Just 15 cm of fast-flowing water can sweep you off your feet.)

> Homes are flooded. Floors and furniture are ruined. Wiring gets damaged – so you could get an electric shock.

> Farm animals get drowned.

> Crops are ruined. In poor countries that could mean people will starve.

> Floodwater can spread diseases. For example **typhoid** often follows flooding in poorer countries.

> Roads may get washed away.

> Shops and offices get flooded. Business comes to a halt. Schools close.

> Cars may get swept away and their engines ruined.

> If sewage systems get flooded, drinking water may get contaminated by sewage. You will feel very ill, and vomit.

The **flood plain** is the area around the river that is likely to flood.

The more people there are living and working on the flood plain, the more damage a flood will do.

Your turn

1 These sentences explain how a flood occurs. They are in the wrong order. Write them in the correct order.
   - The river fills up with water.
   - The ground gets soaked.
   - More rain runs over the ground and into the river.
   - Heavy rain falls for a long period.
   - The water rises over the banks.
   - Infiltration slows down.

2 a Draw a spider map to show the factors that increase the risk of flooding. Like this:

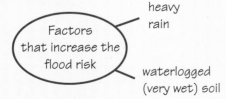

   b Now underline the 'natural' factors in one colour and the 'human' factors in another.

3 Explain these facts about floods.
   a Your home may not be safe to live in for weeks.
   b After a flood, it is a good idea to boil tap water before you drink it.
   c The effect of a flood may last for years.
   d Repairing flood damage can cost millions.

4 The photo above was taken on the outskirts of Peterborough at Easter 1998. The river is the Nene.

   a The photo shows many flooded buildings. What kind of buildings do they seem to be?
   b They have been built in the Nene's flood plain. A lot of building goes on in flood plains. Why do you think that is? Is it a good idea? Explain.
   c The building marked ● is your home. Write an e-mail to a friend in Canada telling her how the water came in, and how you reacted. For example did you try to save anything? Did you ring anyone? What happened next?

Floods in the UK, 2000

In this unit you'll see how, and why, flooding affected one UK town.

Wet wet wet !

Autumn 2000 was the wettest autumn in the UK since records began, over 270 years ago.

It started to rain in September, and rained heavily for over 7 weeks. The ground got soggy. The rivers filled fast. There were floods in 700 locations. And:

◆ 11 000 families had to leave their homes

◆ 10 000 homes and businesses were flooded

◆ over £1.3 billion of damage was done.

Along the River Severn, several towns were badly flooded. Shrewsbury was one of them.

What's Shrewsbury like ?

Shrewsbury is an old and historic town. Many of its buildings date from the Middle Ages. Its population is around 100 000.

Most of the old town centre is in a loop of the River Severn. (Look at the OS map.) This adds to the town's appeal – and to the flood risk. Once every 10 years, on average, floods causes severe damage.

In Autumn 2000, the town had its worst floods in over fifty years. Turn to page 82 to see how it looked.

The River Severn flowing through Shrewsbury

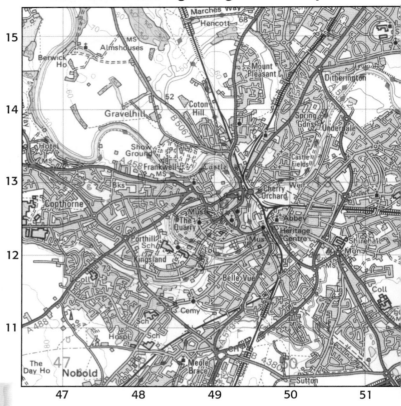

Scale 1: 50 000

Shrewsbury under water

As the biscuits and tea-bags floated past his ankles, Tom Burns decided it was time to close up shop.

Tom is just one of thousands who suffered as the River Severn flooded onto the streets of Shrewsbury. By this morning much of the town was under water, and traffic could not get through.

Many people have left their flooded homes and gone to stay with friends and relatives. Some have been moved into a rescue centre. Some have been given rooms, for free, in hotels in the town.

'I'm glad nobody drowned,' said Sheila Nelson. 'But I hate to think what my house is like now. When I left, the water in the living room was already a foot deep. It was slopping around the TV. Carpets and everything will be ruined. It will take months to put right.'

Adapted from a local newspaper, 2 November 2000.

▲ *Just floating off the shelves.*

So whose fault is it?

'We can't just blame the rain,' said an expert. 'This is a wake-up call for all of us.'

'First, we are causing climate change by burning so much fossil fuel. So we can expect more rain and more storms – and more floods like this one.'

'And second, we are making things much worse by building on flood plains. In 1997-2000, 11% of the new homes in England were on flood plains – which means they're at risk of flooding. This does not make sense!'

'I think local councils should stop people building on flood plains. And if builders do get permission to build there, they must pay to put flood defences in place.'

Adapted from a newspaper, November 2000.

▲ *Heading for home, in Shrewsbury.*

Did you know?
♦ People began to settle at Shrewsbury around 500 AD.
♦ They settled within the loop of the River Severn, for safety.
♦ Then along came the Normans, in 1074, and built a castle there.

Did you know?
♦ The River Severn is the UK's longest river (354 km).
♦ It rises in the Cambrian Mountains in Wales and flows to the Bristol Channel.

▲ *Tea and comfort in a rescue centre.*

Your turn

1 Look at the OS map of Shrewsbury. What clue(s) does it give that the town might be at risk of flooding?

2 Now look back at the photo on page 82.
 a The building near the lower left corner, marked ●, is a shop. It is at 490126 on the OS map. In which direction was the camera pointing?
 b Is the river to the right, or the left, of the trees?

3 Could these have played a part in the Shrewsbury floods? Give reasons. (Page 84 may help.)
 a It rained for seven weeks before the floods.
 b The River Severn drains a large part of the Cambrian Mountains. (See page 127.)
 c The Cambrians get a lot of rain (page 61.)
 d Several tributaries join the Severn before it reaches Shrewsbury.
 e Over the years there has been more and more building in the flood plain in Shrewsbury.

4 Imagine you are Sheila Nelson (from page 86). What will you have to do when you go home, to get your house back to normal?
 a Write a list of tasks. (Think of at least eight.)
 b Put them in order, with the most urgent first.
 c Beside each, write how long you think the work will take, and how much you think it will cost.

5 Imagine you are Tom Burns (from page 86). Write a letter to the local council saying:
 ◆ how the floods have affected you, and
 ◆ what you think should be done to protect Shrewsbury in the future.

6 *'Floods are a natural hazard, but we make them worse.'*
 a Give three ways in which we do that.
 b Suggest things we could do to reduce our impact on flooding. Give your answer as bullet points.

Floods in Bangladesh, 2004

In this unit you'll find out why Bangladesh suffers so much flooding.

Death toll reaches 500 as floods cover Bangladesh

The death toll for this year's floods in Bangladesh has now reached 500. After three weeks of the worst flooding in 15 years, over two-thirds of the country is under water.

Heavy monsoon rains in Bangladesh and its neighbours have caused the country's three big rivers to flood at the same time.

In Dhaka, thousands of people waded through dirty water, looking for safety in a high-rise building, or a school, or a flood shelter. 'This is bad' said Fatima Begum, as she struggled to carry her two children. 'The floods got into the sewage system and now there's sewage everywhere. It has polluted the water supply so we've no clean water. I am so worried my childen will fall ill.'

Water is one problem. Food is another – it is getting harder and harder to find. And the live cables that dangle everywhere add extra danger.

Out in the countryside, all is misery. Reeza Lal and his family huddle under an old plastic sheet on a muddy embankment. Below them, in the swirling river, the swollen bodies of dead cows and chickens bob along in the water, along with tin bowls, and roof beams, and broken furniture.

'I don't know what to do,' said Reeza. 'We have no food, or water. We don't know when we can go home again. My crops have been washed away. My animals have drowned. We have lost everything.'

From newspaper reports, 30 July 2004

Flood factfile

Duration: 1 month
Final death toll: over 600 people
Homeless: over 7 million people
Destroyed or badly damaged:
  2.6 million homes
  11 000 schools
  3000 bridges
  30 000 km of roads
  2 million hectares of crops
Cost of damage: £4 billion

Did you know?
◆ Bangladesh gets nearly 3 times as much rain as the UK a year, on average.

▲ They rescued all they could, from their flooded home.

▲ The floodwaters rise in the streets of Dhaka.

Why are there so many floods in Bangladesh?

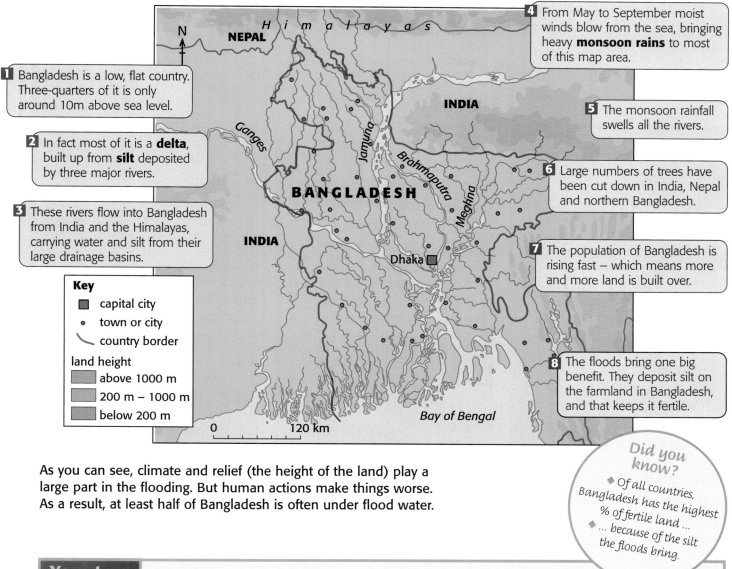

4 From May to September moist winds blow from the sea, bringing heavy **monsoon rains** to most of this map area.

1 Bangladesh is a low, flat country. Three-quarters of it is only around 10m above sea level.

2 In fact most of it is a **delta**, built up from **silt** deposited by three major rivers.

3 These rivers flow into Bangladesh from India and the Himalayas, carrying water and silt from their large drainage basins.

5 The monsoon rainfall swells all the rivers.

6 Large numbers of trees have been cut down in India, Nepal and northern Bangladesh.

7 The population of Bangladesh is rising fast – which means more and more land is built over.

8 The floods bring one big benefit. They deposit silt on the farmland in Bangladesh, and that keeps it fertile.

Key

- ■ capital city
- • town or city
- ⌒ country border

land height
- above 1000 m
- 200 m – 1000 m
- below 200 m

0   120 km

Bay of Bengal

As you can see, climate and relief (the height of the land) play a large part in the flooding. But human actions make things worse. As a result, at least half of Bangladesh is often under flood water.

Did you know?
- ◆ Of all countries, Bangladesh has the highest % of fertile land ...
- ◆ ... because of the silt the floods bring.

Your turn

1 Where in the world is Bangladesh? Which country surrounds it?

2 Bangladesh is a *delta*. What does that mean? (Glossary?)

3 Bangladesh has a huge flood problem. See if you can explain the part each of these plays:
  a It is in the drainage basin of three major rivers.
  b It is low and flat.
  c Rain is not spread evenly through the year. Most falls in a 5-month period.
  d The population nearly doubled between 1975 and 2005.
  e 2 billion tonnes of silt are carried into Bangladesh each year, and most is deposited on the river beds.

4 Overall, Bangladesh has a far higher risk of flooding than the UK does. Give at least three reasons to explain why.

5 After floods in Bangladesh, millions of people suffer for months, or even years. Below are some reasons for this. Copy and complete them in your own words.
  a Many houses are flimsy, so ...
  b Many people have no savings, so ...
  c Many farmers lose all their crops, so ...
  d There is just one doctor for every 4300 people, so ...

6 'Flood victims in Bangladesh suffer more than flood victims in the UK.' Do you agree? Give reasons for your answer.

Coping with floods

In this unit you'll compare how the UK and Bangladesh cope with flooding, and try to explain the differences.

How does the UK cope?

In England and Wales, the Environment Agency looks after rivers.

They build flood defences in areas at high risk – like these raised banks or **embankments**.

They check water height and flow to see if a river is going to flood. (There are meters in this hut.)

They work with the weather people and police to warn us – by radio, TV, phone, or knocking on doors.

Local people also help themselves. For example by putting down sandbags to keep the water out.

The **emergency services** – fire brigade, police and army – spring into action when needed.

Organizations like the Red Cross, and local shops, and schools, help the victims with food and shelter.

But flood defences cost a lot. We can't build them everywhere. So floods in the UK can still do a great deal of damage.

Comparing the UK and Bangladesh

The UK is more **developed** than most countries. That means people have a good standard of living, overall.

The country has a good **infrastructure** (roads, phone system, water supply, electricity supply and so on). And most people have enough money to live on.

Bangladesh is less developed, as you can see from this table. The infrastructure is poor. 90% of the roads are not paved – they are just dirt tracks. Many people live in great poverty.

There are many reasons for these differences. You will learn about them later in your course.

Comparing the UK and Bangladesh		
	UK	**Bangladesh**
Population (millions)	59	136
Area (sq km)	243 000	144 000
Number of people/ per sq km	244	1042
Average amount people earn a year	£18 600	£124
The % of people living in rural areas	10%	84%
Length of paved roads per 1000 sq km of land	1531 km	138 km
Number of phone lines per 1000 people	587	4
Number of radios per 1000 people	1406	45
Number of TVs per 1000 people	508	6

How does Bangladesh cope?

Bangladesh has much worse flooding than the UK. How does it cope?

Many buildings – like this house – are built on stilts to protect them from floods.

There are hundreds of km of embankments. They keep people safe – but they are not everywhere.

There is a warning system – but it is hard to warn the people in rural areas.

When floods arrive, the police and army do what they can – but they can't be everywhere.

Some flood shelters are built – but not nearly enough. People shelter wherever they can.

After bad floods they need help from the rest of the world: food, tents, seeds, medicine, money.

Your turn

1 a Which organization looks after rivers, in England?
  b What are *emergency services*?

2 A–C below are some responses to floods in the UK.
  a Which of them do you think are:
    i short-term? ii long-term? (Glossary?)
    A The Environment Agency builds flood defences.
    B The emergency services are always prepared.
    C Neighbours give flood victims a hot meal.
  b Find one more example of each type of response, (short- and long-term) for flooding in the UK.
  c Now see if you can pick out *two* examples of each type of response for Bangladesh.

3 In what ways are the responses to flooding in Bangladesh and the UK: a similar? b different?

4 Look at the data in the table on page 90.
  a Give reasons why it's harder to warn people about floods in Bangladesh than in the UK.
  b Explain why it's harder to get help to flood victims in Bangladesh.
  c Explain why more people suffer in Bangladesh than in the UK, when a river floods.

5 *'The richer and more developed a country is, the better it can cope with floods and other disasters.'* Do you agree? Explain in *not less than* 50 words.

6 Overall, the UK copes well with floods. But suppose half the country is under water for weeks (as in Bangladesh). How would we cope then? Describe what your life might be like by week 4.

Flood control

In this unit, you'll learn about ways to prevent floods.

How can we control or prevent floods?

When rivers flood, we help the victims with shelter and food. But that's a short-term solution. We also try to prevent floods in the future. Here are four ways to do that:

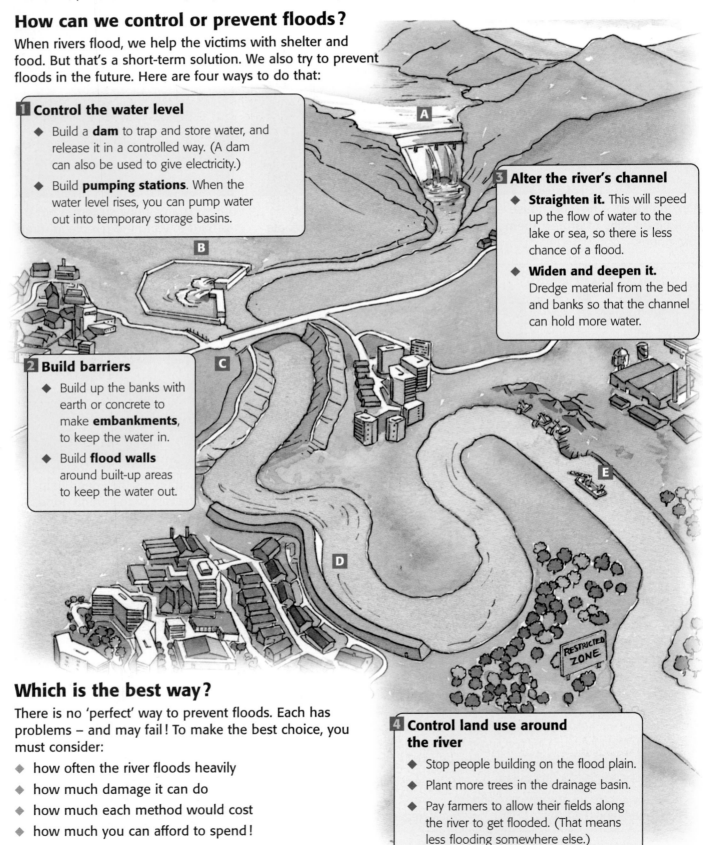

1 Control the water level

◆ Build a **dam** to trap and store water, and release it in a controlled way. (A dam can also be used to give electricity.)

◆ Build **pumping stations**. When the water level rises, you can pump water out into temporary storage basins.

2 Build barriers

◆ Build up the banks with earth or concrete to make **embankments**, to keep the water in.

◆ Build **flood walls** around built-up areas to keep the water out.

3 Alter the river's channel

◆ **Straighten it.** This will speed up the flow of water to the lake or sea, so there is less chance of a flood.

◆ **Widen and deepen it.** Dredge material from the bed and banks so that the channel can hold more water.

4 Control land use around the river

◆ Stop people building on the flood plain.

◆ Plant more trees in the drainage basin.

◆ Pay farmers to allow their fields along the river to get flooded. (That means less flooding somewhere else.)

Which is the best way?

There is no 'perfect' way to prevent floods. Each has problems – and may fail! To make the best choice, you must consider:

◆ how often the river floods heavily

◆ how much damage it can do

◆ how much each method would cost

◆ how much you can afford to spend!

Some disadvantages

◆ Floods deposit silt on fields in the flood plain. This keeps soil fertile. So if you prevent flooding, the soil gets less fertile.
That would be a big problem in Bangladesh, where farmers depend on the silt and can't afford fertilizer.

◆ Embankments in one place can cause worse flooding elsewhere. (Water has to go somewhere!)

◆ Changes to a river will drive wildlife away.

▲ Up go the demountable flood barriers, in Shrewsbury in 2002. They'll be taken down again when this flood recedes.

Your turn

1 Look at the drawing on page 92.
   a Name the features at A, B, C and D, and say what job each does.
   b What is going on at E? How can this prevent floods?

2 The four blue panels show four different approaches to flood prevention. Which approach do you think:
   a costs most?   b is best for wildlife?
   c costs least?   d is best for the river's appearance?
   e is the most sustainable? (Glossary?)
   Give reasons for your answers.

3 After the floods in 2000, the Environment Agency drew up plans to protect Shrewsbury (page 86).
   You have to guess *why* it turned down each idea **A–D** below. Answer as fully as you can, using what you've learned so far – and the extra clues in the clue box!
   A Dredge the river.
   B Build a channel to cut off the river loop during floods. (See the dotted lines on the map below.)
   C Build high flood walls all along the loop.
   D Build a dam upstream.

4 In the end the Environment Agency decided on demountable flood barriers for the Frankwell area.
   a What are *demountable barriers*? (Photo!)
   b Why are they a good idea for Shrewsbury?
   c Why did it choose Frankwell as a key area to protect? (Check out the maps on page 86 and below.)

5 Your job is to try to control flooding in Bangladesh. Your options are:
   ① Build dams in Northern Bangladesh.
   ② Move everyone off the flood plains.
   ③ Build embankments all the way along the rivers.
   ④ Build embankments just around towns and cities.
   ⑤ Build pumping stations all along the rivers.
   ⑥ Plant lots of trees in Bangladesh.
   ⑦ Dredge the rivers, and use the sediment to build higher land where people can live safely.
   ⑧ Straighten the rivers.
   ⑨ Ask India and Nepal to plant lots of trees.
   You can choose more than one option.

   a First, go through the options. Decide whether each will work or not, and say why.
   The map on page 89 will help you decide.
   b Now write a report for the Bangladeshi government. It should have three parts:
   ◆ What you plan to do.
   ◆ How well it is likely to work. (Will it stop all flooding? What are the drawbacks?)
   ◆ What else should to be done to protect people. (Think about housing, flood shelters and so on.)
   You can use drawings to make your plan clear.

Clue box

The bridges would get in the way. And once you start you have to keep on doing this!	Farmland would have to be drowned to build this – and it could cause floods in villages upstream.

The river view is a big part of Shrewsbury's appeal.

Would need a huge tunnel under roads, the railway, and people's land. Cost: up to £100 million!

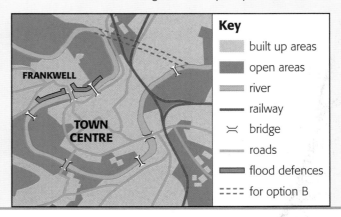

Key

▨	built up areas
▨	open areas
▨	river
—	railway
⋈	bridge
—	roads
▬	flood defences
====	for option B

FRANKWELL

TOWN CENTRE

The big picture

Geography is brilliant – it even covers sport! This chapter takes football as an example. These are the big ideas behind the chapter:

◆ Football links people and places all around the world.

◆ It's fun – but it's also big business, and lots of people depend on it for a living (not just the players).

◆ Some earn a fortune from it. But people in poorer countries who make the kit get paid very little.

◆ A football stadium can have a big impact on its surroundings.

These ideas apply to many other sports too.

Did you know?
◆ Around 200 BC in China, 'football' meant kicking a leather ball, filled with hair and feathers, through an opening less than 50 cm wide.

Your goals for this chapter

By the end of this chapter you should be able to answer these questions:

◆ In what ways does football link people and places around the world?

◆ Are the UK's most successful teams in the biggest towns and cities? If so, why is this?

◆ What do these terms mean?

economic activity   primary sector   secondary sector   tertiary sector

◆ What kinds of jobs are linked to football?

◆ Why is football described as big business?

◆ What kind of impact does a stadium have on an area?

◆ When clubs move stadiums, who gains and who may lose out?

◆ Why is so much of the sports kit sold here made in poorer countries?

Did you know?
◆ In 1314 the Mayor of London banned football in the city, because it caused such a rumpus.
◆ People caught playing it could be sent to prison.

And then …

When you finish the chapter, come back to this page and see if you have met your goals!

Did you know?
◆ Football is now the top sport played by girls and women in the UK.

Your chapter starter

Football is just geography in action!

Look at the photo on page 94.

The ball was made in Pakistan, and the boots in India. The match will be wached on TV in Nigeria, and Japan, and many other countries.

What other links can you find to geography, in the photo? Come up with as many as you can.

Come on my son!

Exploring success in football

In this unit you'll explore some reasons why some teams – and some countries – are more successful at football than others.

The football winners

▲ *World Cup winners, 2002: Brazil*

▲ *Olympic Football champions, 2004: USA*

Every club, and every country, likes to win at football.

So why do some do better than others? Is it just about talent? Or the size of a place? Or is it all down to wealth? It's up to you to explore!

Your turn

First, get warmed up

1 Your task is to match each dot on the map to the correct team from the list below.

Sheffield Wednesday
Newcastle United
Manchester United
Cardiff City
Liverpool
Brighton
Arsenal
Blackpool
Hull City
Celtic

Write your answer like this: A = _____
(And no foul play or you'll be sent off!)

2 Football teams are in different **leagues**, depending on how good they are. Name as many leagues for England and Wales as you can, in order, best first.

Is success linked to the size of a place?

3 Do bigger cities tend to have better football teams? It's time to find out. The first table on page 97 shows 24 towns and cities in England and Wales (outside London) with teams in the top four leagues.
   a Which is the *largest* city or town in the list *without* a team in the Premier League?
   b Which is the *smallest* city or town *with* a team in the Premier League?

4 a Now make a large copy of the scattergraph started below. (Use graph paper if you can. Use a full page, turned sideways.) Put in all the lines shown here.

UK city or town	Population (thousands)	Team(s)	League (2004–05)
Birmingham	977	Aston Villa	Premier
		Birmingham City	Premier
Blackpool	142	Blackpool	One
Bournemouth	163	Bournemouth	One
Cardiff	305	Cardiff City	Championship
Darlington	98	Darlington	Two
Derby	289	Derby County	Championship
Ipswich	117	Ipswich Town	Championship
Leicester	280	Leicester City	Championship
Liverpool	439	Liverpool	Premier
		Everton	Premier
Luton	184	Luton Town	One
Macclesfield	150	Macclesfield Town	Two
Manchester	393	Manchester United	Premier
		Manchester City	Premier
Northampton	194	Northampton Town	Two
Oldham	217	Oldham Athletic	One
Oxford	134	Oxford United	Two
Peterborough	156	Peterborough United	One
Portsmouth	187	Portsmouth	Premier
Sheffield	513	Sheffield United	Championship
		Sheffield Wednesday	One
Shrewsbury	100	Shrewsbury Town	Two
Southampton	217	Southampton	Premier
Southend	160	Southend United	Two
Swindon	180	Swindon Town	One
Walsall	253	Walsall	One
Wolverhampton	234	Wolverhampton Wanderers	Championship

b Complete your graph for all 24 places in the table. Then make up a title for it.

c Look at your scattergraph. Does it show a link between the population of places and the success of their teams? Describe any *overall* trend you can see.

d Try to think up reasons to explain this trend.

5 a Now draw a larger copy of this flowchart.

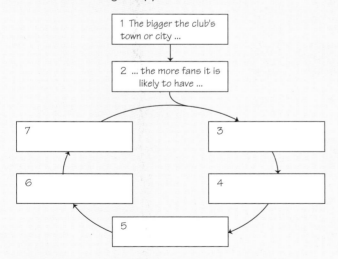

1 The bigger the club's town or city ...

2 ... the more fans it is likely to have ...

7

3

6

4

5

b Write in the five part-sentences below in the right boxes, to complete the flowchart. (One per box.)

...so then it can buy in more good players...

...so it can sell more match tickets...

...so it will win more matches...

...so it will get more fans...

...which means it will make more money...

c Look at your completed flowchart for **b**. Does it help to explain the pattern you found in **4**?

d Do you agree with the logic in your flowchart? Give it a mark out of 10.

Are poorer countries less successful at football?

6 *'Poorer countries are not as successful as richer countries, at football.'*
Do you agree? Answer *Yes*, *No* or *Not sure*.

7 The table below shows the 2004 world football rankings for some countries, and the average wealth per person in these countries (in US dollars).

Country	FIFA ranking in 2004	Average wealth per person (in US$)
Argentina	5	10 000
Brazil	1	8000
Cameroon	12	2000
Croatia	42	9000
England	17	25 000
France	2	26 000
Germany	8	27 000
Italy	10	25 000
Japan	23	28 000
Kenya	79	1000
Mali	46	900
Morocco	33	4000
Niger	170	800
Nigeria	16	900
United States	9	38 000

a In which one of these countries are people richest, on average? In which are they poorest?

b Now draw a scattergraph for the data in the table. You will need *long* axes. Label them as started here:

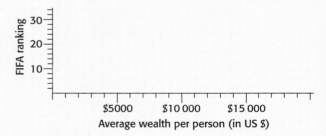

c Study your scattergraph. Then answer question **6** again – and this time give your evidence.

d Can you suggest anything further you could do, to check for links between wealth and success in football? (The world has over 200 countries!)

8 Look again at the table above. Use it to explain why:

a some top Brazilian players have joined English teams

b players from England don't join Brazilian teams.

Earning a living from football

In this unit you'll learn about the different jobs that are linked to football.

Jobs in a football club

You don't have to play football to get a job in a football club! Look at these:

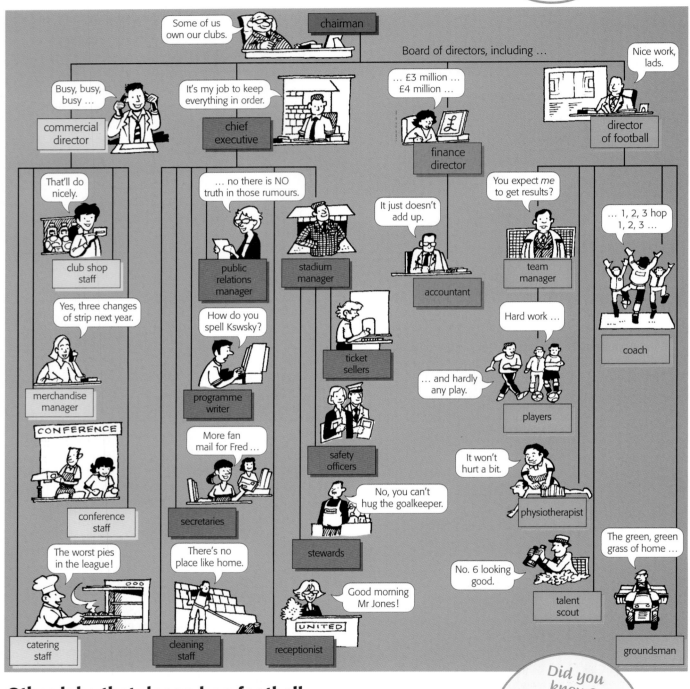

Other jobs that depend on football

Hundreds of other jobs *outside* the clubs also depend on football. Like these:

- sewing football strip (the kit the players wear)
- writing about football for a newspaper
- running the football pools.

Your turn

1 Look at the drawing of the football club on page 98.
   a Who is in charge of the players?
      See if you can name one real person with this job.
   b What do the catering staff do?
   c What does a physiotherapist do?
   d What does the groundsman do?
   e Explain what a board of directors is, in your
      own words.

2 *Economic activity* means work you get paid for.
   (You may have met this on page 66.)
   It can be divided into four kinds or **sectors**:

primary – you collect things from the Earth. Farming, fishing, mining.

secondary – you make or **manufacture** things. Like shoes, chairs, paint.

tertiary – you provide **services**. Like teach, or look after sick people.

quaternary – you do **hi-tech** work. Like develop new drugs to cure disease.

Now look again at the jobs in the football club.
   a Are any of them in the quaternary sector?
   b Do any belong to the primary or secondary sectors?
      (Did you have any problem deciding? If so, why?)
   c Overall, what can you say about jobs in a football club?

3 a Now draw a large spider map to show jobs *outside*
      the club that are linked to football. Give as many as
      you can. You could start like this:

football writer

Jobs that are linked to football (outside the club)

strip designer

   b On your spider map, underline any primary sector
      jobs in one colour, secondary in another, and so on.
      Add a key to explain the colours.

4 This is the story of replica football strip:

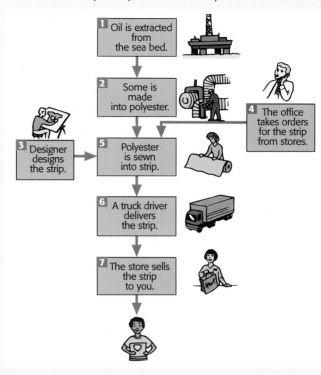

1 Oil is extracted from the sea bed.

2 Some is made into polyester.

3 Designer designs the strip.

4 The office takes orders for the strip from stores.

5 Polyester is sewn into strip.

6 A truck driver delivers the strip.

7 The store sells the strip to you.

   a Make your own copy of the flowchart.
      (Leave out the drawings!)
   b Now underline any primary activities in one
      colour, secondary in another colour, and so on.
   c Add a key to show what the colours mean.

5 Lots of people earn a living from football – but some
   earn more than others! This shows pay in one club:

Job	Pay per year
cleaner	£10 000
catering manager	£36 000
coach	£85 000
stadium manager	£60 000
player	£250 000
team manager	£100 000
secretary	£24 000

   a Draw a bar chart to show this data.
      (Turn your graph paper sideways?)
      Show the pay in order, starting with the largest.
   b The player earns ___ times as much as the
      cleaner. What's the missing number?
   c Do you think he works ___ times as hard as
      the cleaner?
   d Do you think this big difference in pay is fair?
      Give reasons.

In this unit you'll learn how the big football clubs earn money – and how good players and stadiums help.

It's big business

Football is not just a game – it is big business. The top clubs earn, and spend, millions of pounds a year. These photos give clues about how they earn money. (You will have to match the numbers to words later.)

How clubs spend money

- paying the players
- paying other staff
- buying new players
- improving stadiums
- hosting matches
- going to away matches
- training youth teams
- working with schools

Now look at the list on the right. It shows how clubs spend money. Some get into trouble because they spend more than they earn!

And not just for the clubs

It's not just the big football clubs that make money from football.

Local shops, cafes, pubs and restaurants are all busier than usual on match days.

▶ *They'll be ever so hungry and thirsty after this.*

Your turn

How a big football club makes money

Way of making money	Could the club earn more from this by ...	
	having better players?	moving to a bigger, better stadium?
❶ selling match tickets		yes
❷		

1 These are ways a big football club makes money:
  ◆ selling match tickets
  ◆ catering (bars and restaurants)
  ◆ selling merchandise (strip, scarves, and so on)
  ◆ TV fees (for matches shown on TV)
  ◆ renting out rooms for conferences
  ◆ renting out private viewing boxes
  ◆ sponsorship

  You have to match them to the numbers 1–7 in the photos on page 100. Here is what to do.
  a Make a table with headings like the one above. Extend it to show rows numbered 1–7.
  b Write the correct items in column 2, to match the numbers in column 1. (Pick from the list above.)
  c Do you think a club will sell more tickets if it has better players? Write *yes* or *no* in row 1, column 3.
  d Fill in column 3 for all the other rows.
  e Now decide if moving stadiums will affect what the club can earn for each item, and fill in the last column.

2 Draw a spider map to show who else gains when a football club is successful. You could start like this:

3 Like every business, football clubs need to make money. Many buy players from all over the world, to help them do that. This will show how it works:

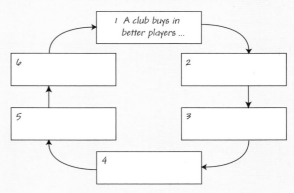

Make a larger copy of the flowchart.
Then write these in the correct boxes ...
  ... so it can afford more of the world's top players.
  ... which means it sells more tickets and more merchandise.
  So the club gets richer and richer...
  ... so it wins more and more matches...
  This also means it makes more money from TV and sponsorship.

4 And finally, back to stadiums. Around the UK, many clubs have moved to new stadiums, or are thinking about it. Using your table for 1 to help you, write a paragraph to explain why.

In this unit you will learn about Arsenal's move to its new stadium – and explore the impact of the move.

It's all go for the Gunners!

In 1913, Arsenal played its first game at Highbury. In 2006, 93 years later, it will play its first game at its new home in Ashburton Grove.

'We're sad to leave Highbury,' said manager Arsene Wenger. 'But we must, if we want to grow. Highbury held only 38 500 people. The new stadium will hold 60 000. It will bring in a lot more money – and the fans will be happy to see more tickets on sale.

Not just a stadium

It's not just a stadium. The redevelopment at Ashburton Grove includes:

- 2000 new or improved homes
- space for shops and other businesses
- a new sports and community centre for the local people
- 2 new gyms
- 4 community health centres.

Arsenal promises that the redevelopment will bring 1800 new jobs to the area. But it has not all been plain sailing. Many local people objected to Arsenal's plans. Two even went to the High Court to fight them!

Letters to the editor

Dear Sir

Now that Arsenal have had their way, we are doomed. 60 000 fans will descend on us every 10 days or so. How will we cope?

The fans are not my only complaint. I ran a business on the Ashburton Grove site – until the council forced me to move, to make way for the stadium!

Why should people like me get pushed out, just because a greedy football club wants to make more money? It's not fair.

I have always hated football. Now it has ruined my life.

Yours in disgust

Bill Simmonds

Your turn

1 What was the main reason for Arsenal's move?

2 When the club first talked about moving, the fans made lots of suggestions. Here are two:

Give reasons why the club said no to each.

3 a Make a table with headings like the one below.

Finding a new site for a football stadium	
Things to think about	Score for Ashburton Grove
Large enough?	
Close to public transport?	
Near our fans?	

b In the first column, list all the things you'd think about, if you had to find a new site for a stadium.

c In the second column, give Ashburton Grove a score for each thing. (0 = poor, 5 = excellent.)

4 Look at the aerial photo on page 103. In which direction was the camera pointing?

5 The local council forced Arsenal to build some things to help the local people, in return for permission to use the site. See if you can identify them from the list above.

6 a Make a large table like the one started below. You could use a new page, turned sideways.

The impact of the Ashburton Grove redevelopment			
on Arsenal FC		on the local people	
positive	negative	positive	negative
....	....	....	....

b Now complete the table. Under *positive* write the benefits. Under *negative* write the bad points. Try to think of everything. For example what will the effect be on traffic? On the tube stations?

c Overall:

i Has Arsenal FC gained more than it lost?

ii have the local people gained more than they lost?

Arsenal's home area

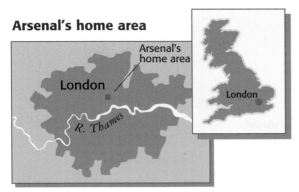

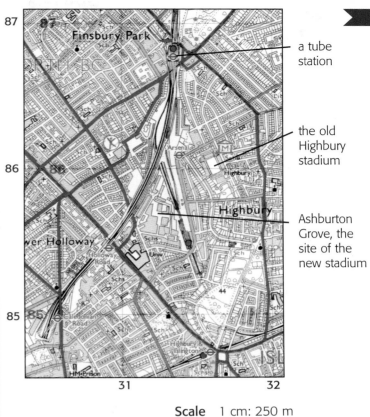

a tube station

the old Highbury stadium

Ashburton Grove, the site of the new stadium

Scale   1 cm: 250 m

▲ *An OS map (2002) showing the sites of the old and new stadiums. They are just a short walk apart.*

Some of the Highbury stands will be turned into flats. The pitch will be planted with trees.

Some of this site was waste ground – but not all. Over 60 businesses had to move, to make way for the new stadium.

◀ *The new stadium being built at Ashburton Grove, in 2004. Look at the old Highbury stadium in the background.*

◀ *The new development around the stadium.*

◀ *The new stadium at Ashburton Grove.*

Who are the losers?

In this unit you'll learn how some 'football' workers are paid very unfairly.

Football skills

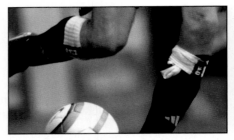

This player earned around £1500 today for kicking this ball.
(He scored a goal, with great skill.)

The football is made of rubber and synthetic leather. It is top quality. It could cost £65 in the shops.

It was sewn by hand, with great skill, by Omar, aged 14. It took him 3 hours. He got paid 65p.

Omar lives on the outskirts of Sialkot in Pakistan.

In that city, and the villages around it, they make 75% of the world's hand-stitched footballs. They produce an amazing 35 million footballs a year.

A vicious circle

Why is Omar paid so little? This is what happens:

This British company supplies footballs. It gets them made …

… and then sells them to clubs and sports shops at a profit.

We must make more profit …

The less it pays for the footballs the more profit it will make …

… so it searches the world for a factory to make them cheaply.

The footballs are shipped to the UK. They have been well made. The British company is happy.

But what can we do?

They can't leave because they need the work. If they don't have jobs they will starve.

That's the best I can offer.

He also wants to make as much profit as he can. So he pays his workers very little.

That's the best I can offer.

This factory owner in Sialkot wants the work – but if he charges too much he won't get it.

It's not just British companies. It happens in all the richer countries.
They get things made in poorer countries where wages are lower.
Not just footballs, but football strip, and boots, and other sports items.
You will find out more about this later in your course.

Omar's story

I have been sewing footballs since I was 8.

I don't like it much. But I have to do it, because my dad died and we need the money. My mum used to sew too but now she has trouble with her eyes. So I have to support my family.

I work in a stitching centre. I start at 7 in the morning and often work till 8 in the evening. I do 4 footballs a day – so I earn £2.60 a day. But they can throw me out any time. I don't know what I will do if that happens.

I get tired of sewing all day. My shoulders get stiff. My eyes get sore. My fingers are all cut. I would love to go to school instead – but no chance!

I saw a World Cup match on the TV at my uncle's house. The football could have been one I sewed. But nobody at the match knew about me!

▲ *Omar at work.*

1 A certain Premier League footballer earns £15 000 a week. (The really big stars earn a lot more.) How long would Omar have to work to earn that much?

2 Suppose you buy a football for £50, made in Sialkot. Where does the money go? It could go like this:

	£
The shop where you bought it	10.00
The British supplier	31.00
Shipping and transport companies	1.50
The Sialkot factory owner	5.00
The company that supplied the materials for the football	1.50
The stitcher	0.50
Other factory costs (lighting etc)	0.50
Total	**£50.00**

What percentage of the money does the factory owner get? You can work it out like this:

$$\frac{\text{factory owner's share}}{\text{total amount}} \times 100\%$$

$$= \frac{£5}{£50} \times 100 = 10\%$$

a Now work out the percentages for the others in the list.

b Draw a pie chart to show how the money is shared.

c Who gets: the largest share? the smallest?

3 Look at the 'vicious circle' on page 104. What might happen if:

a the stitchers went on strike?

b the factory manager tried to charge the British company more?

c the British company charged the shops more?

d everyone refused to use footballs made in Pakistan?

e someone invented a machine that could sew footballs perfectly?

4 In some ways, Omar's life is also a vicious circle.

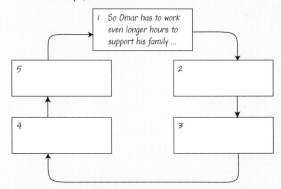

Make a larger copy of the drawing above, Then write the following in the correct boxes.

… but every year food and clothes cost a little more …

… so he can't get a better-paid job …

… so he has even less chance to go to school …

… so he can't learn new skills (like reading and writing) …

5 How would you make life less unfair for the stitchers? Give your answer in not less than 150 words.

Plates, earthquakes and volcanoes

The big picture

This chapter is all about earthquakes and volcanoes, and the huge slabs or **plates** that the Earth's crust is broken into. These are the big ideas in the chapter:

◆ Earthquakes and volcanic eruptions have killed millions of people, and ruined millions of lives.

◆ They are caused by currents of hot soft rock inside the Earth, which drag the Earth's plates around.

◆ We can't stop them. All we can do is help the survivors, and find ways to protect people in the future.

◆ This can cost a lot of money. But poor countries don't have much, so they may need help from other countries.

Your goals for this chapter

By the end of this chapter you should be able to answer these questions:

◆ What do these terms mean?

*crust   mantle   core   lithosphere   convection current
oceanic crust   continental crust*

◆ What are the Earth's plates, and why do they move?

◆ What causes earthquakes, and what damage do they do?

◆ What do these terms mean?

fault   focus   epicentre   seismic wave   aftershock

◆ What are volcanoes, and what damage do eruptions do?

◆ What do these terms mean?

magma   lava   crater   pyroclastic flow   mudflow   ash

◆ What's the link between plates, earthquakes, and volcanoes?

◆ How do humans respond to earthquakes and eruptions?

◆ Why might these events be more disastrous in poor countries?

◆ Why do people continue to live in danger zones?

And then …

When you finish the chapter, come back to this page and see if you have met your goals!

Did you know?
◆ You are living on a moving slab of rock.
◆ It's moving at about the speed your nails grow!

Did you know?
◆ China is the worst place in the world for earthquake deaths.
◆ In 1556, one earthquake in China killed 830 000 people.

Did you know?
◆ The UK has 200–300 earthquakes a year.
◆ Most are so small that people don't feel them.

Did you know?
◆ There is more volcanic activity under the oceans than on land!

Did you know?
◆ The country with most volcanoes is Indonesia.

Your chapter starter

Look at the photo on page 106. What do you think happened here?

Could anyone have stopped it?

How do you think the people felt about it?

Where do you think they've gone?

Do you think people will ever come back here to live?

HELP!

A slice through the Earth

In this unit you'll learn about the three layers that make up the Earth – and then take a closer look at the layer you live on!

The three layers that make up the Earth

1 The crust
This is the layer you live on. It is a thin skin of rock around the Earth, like the skin on an apple (shown here by the thin blue line).

2 The mantle
It forms about half of the Earth. It is made of heavier rock.

The upper mantle is hard. But the rock below it is hot and soft, like soft toffee. It is runny in places.

3 The core
It is a mainly iron, mixed with a little nickel. The **outer core** is liquid. The **inner core** is solid.

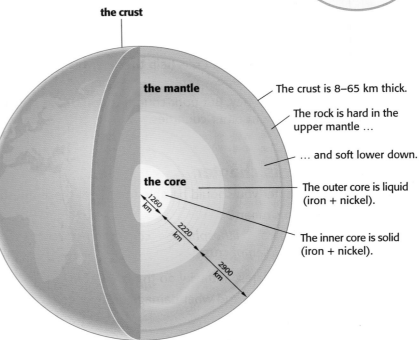

the crust

the mantle

the core

1260 km

2220 km

2900 km

The crust is 8–65 km thick.

The rock is hard in the upper mantle …

… and soft lower down.

The outer core is liquid (iron + nickel).

The inner core is solid (iron + nickel).

How did the layers form?

Some time after the Earth formed, it got so hot that everything inside it melted. The heavier substances in the liquid sank and the lighter ones rose, forming layers. As the Earth cooled, most of the layers turned solid.

Hot hot hot

A great deal of heat is still trapped inside the Earth. That's why it gets hotter as you go down through it. 200 km down, the rocks are glowing white hot. At the centre of the Earth, the temperature is around 5500 °C.

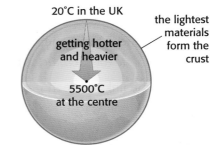

20°C in the UK

getting hotter and heavier

the lightest materials form the crust

5500°C at the centre

▲ A bubble of boiling rock reaching the Earth's surface in Hawaii.

▲ Several countries are digging holes to find out more about the Earth's crust. The deepest is in Russia – over 12 km!

More about the Earth's crust

There are two types of crust. The crust under the oceans is called the **oceanic crust**. It's a thin layer of heavy rock. The **continental crust** is made of lighter rock and forms the continents.

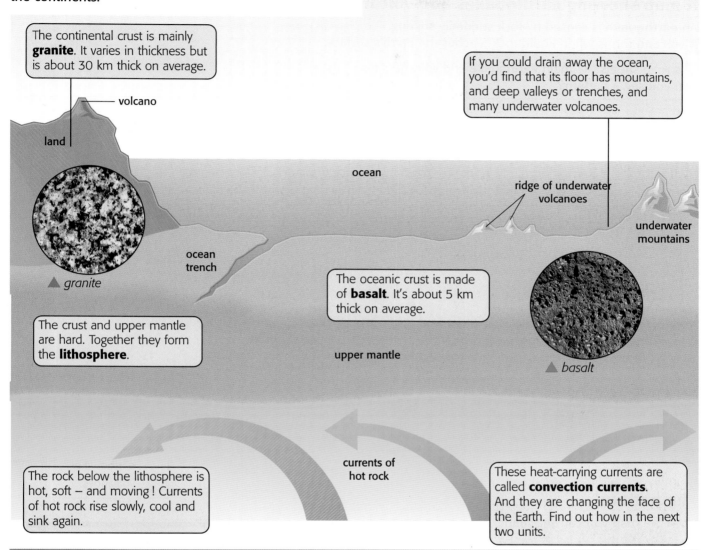

The continental crust is mainly **granite**. It varies in thickness but is about 30 km thick on average.

volcano

land

▲ granite

ocean trench

The crust and upper mantle are hard. Together they form the **lithosphere**.

If you could drain away the ocean, you'd find that its floor has mountains, and deep valleys or trenches, and many underwater volcanoes.

ocean

ridge of underwater volcanoes

underwater mountains

The oceanic crust is made of **basalt**. It's about 5 km thick on average.

upper mantle

▲ basalt

currents of hot rock

The rock below the lithosphere is hot, soft – and moving! Currents of hot rock rise slowly, cool and sink again.

These heat-carrying currents are called **convection currents**. And they are changing the face of the Earth. Find out how in the next two units.

Your turn

1 Make a table like this, and fill it in for the Earth's layers.

Layer	Made of ...	Solid or liquid?	How thick?
crust			
mantle			
core – outer – inner			

2 a What is the Earth's radius, in km, at the thickest part of the crust?

b If you cycle at 20 km an hour, how long will it take you to cycle to the centre of the Earth?

3 Make a larger drawing like this, and complete the labels.

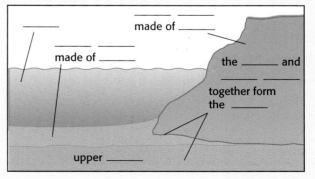

made of _____

made of _____

the _____ and

together form the _____

upper _____

Earthquakes, volcanoes and plates

In this unit you'll learn what the Earth's plates are – and their link with earthquakes and volcanoes.

A map showing earthquakes and volcanoes

An **earthquake** is caused by rock suddenly shifting.
A **volcano** forms when liquid rock reaches the Earth's surface.

This map shows the main earthquake and volcano sites.
Can you see a pattern?

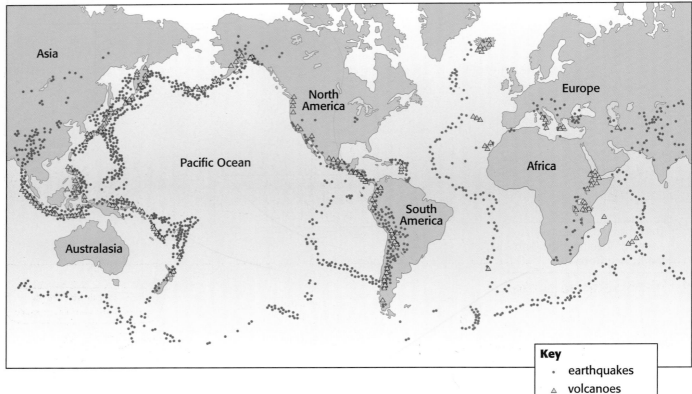

Asia

North America

Europe

Pacific Ocean

Africa

South America

Australasia

Key
- earthquakes
△ volcanoes

The pattern

From the map you can see that:

◆ Earthquakes and volcanoes don't happen just anywhere. They tend to occur along lines.

◆ They often occur together.

◆ They occur in the ocean as well as on land.

Explaining the pattern

The pattern puzzled scientists for years. Then they found the explanation:

◆ The Earth's surface is cracked into pieces, like an eggshell.

◆ The pieces are continually moving.

◆ This movement causes earthquakes and volcanoes along the cracks.

They called the cracked pieces **plates**.

▲ *Research ships like this one helped scientists crack the plate puzzle. They are used to study the ocean floor.*

A map showing the Earth's plates

This map shows the main plates and their names.
Some plates carry continents and ocean, others just
ocean. They move slowly in different directions.

Key
- ∿∿ plate boundary (edge)
- ••••• uncertain plate boundary
- → direction in which plate is moving
- • earthquakes
- △ volcanoes

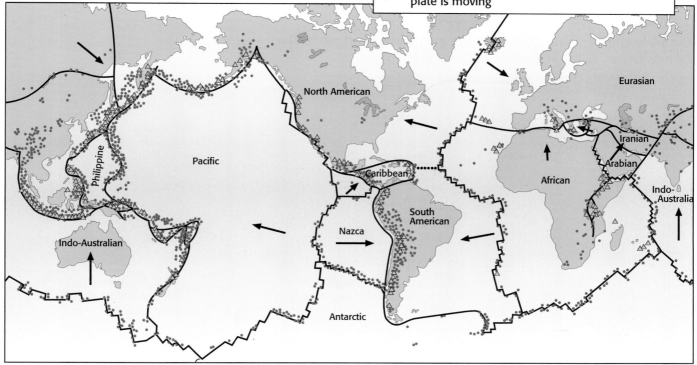

North American
Eurasian
Philippine
Pacific
Iranian
Caribbean
Arabian
African
Indo-Australia
South American
Nazca
Indo-Australian
Antarctic

A closer look at plates

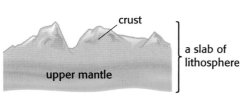

crust
a slab of lithosphere
upper mantle

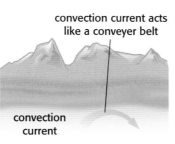

convection current acts like a conveyer belt
convection current

If I just lie still for 10 years I'll move half a metre.

Plates are slabs of the
lithosphere – Earth's crust and
upper mantle. They float on the soft
hot rock below.

Plates move because they are
dragged along by the powerful
convection currents in the soft
hot rock.

Plates move just a few cm a year –
but it all adds up! For example
India has moved 2000 km north in
the last 70 million years.

Your turn

1 Earthquakes and volcanoes tend to form a pattern.
Explain why.

2 Name:
a the plate you live on
b a plate that is moving away from yours
c a plate that is moving north
d a plate that carries just ocean
e the plate off the west coast of South America
f the plate that's circled by the Ring of Fire.

3 Make a drawing of your own to show what plates are
made of and why they move. Give it a snappy title!

4 There are no active volcanoes in the UK. Suggest why.

5 Do you think a map of the Earth will look different
100 million years from now? Explain your answer.

6 A challenge! A move of 1° south equals 440 km.
Suppose our plate starts moving south at 5 cm a year.
About how long will it take Newcastle to reach the
equator? (Newcastle is about 55° N.)

Plate movements

In this unit you'll learn how the Earth's plates are moving – and how their movements produce earthquakes, volcanoes, and even mountains!

1 Some plates are moving apart

Our plate and the North American plate are moving apart, under the Atlantic Ocean. (Look at the map on page 111.)

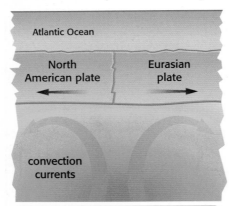 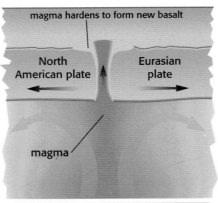 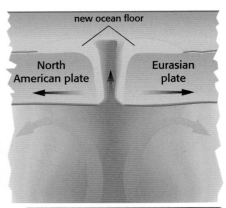

1 The plates are pulled apart by the convection currents in the soft rock below them.

2 Liquid rock or **magma** rises between the plates. It hardens to basalt …

3 … which forms new ocean floor. So the ocean floor is getting wider – by about 2 cm a year.

The rising magma is a form of volcanic eruption. And as the heavy plates move apart, you get earthquakes too! So, whenever plates move apart, you get earthquakes, and eruptions, and new ocean floor being formed.

2 Some plates are pushing into each other

The Nazca plate and the South American plate are pushing into each other, just off the west coast of South America. (Look at the map on page 111.)

The result is earthquakes and volcanoes.

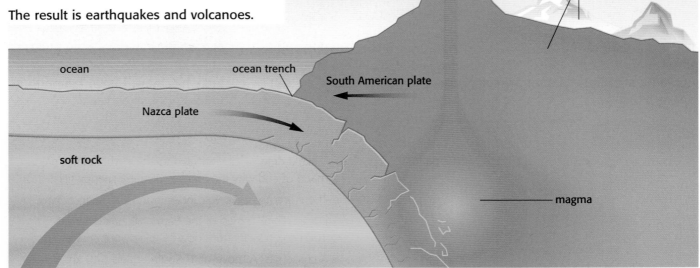

1 The Nazca plate is heavier. (Oceanic crust is heavier.) So it gets pushed under at an ocean trench.

2 The rock jolts and grinds its way down, causing earthquakes. At the same time …

3 … it heats up. Some rock melts, and forces its way up through the Andes to form a volcano.

When pushing makes mountains

Look at these two plates pushing into each other. One carries India, the other China.

Both are continental crust, so this time neither is pushed under. Instead, the crust gets squeezed up to form mountains – the Himalayas.

The plates are still pushing. So the Himalayas are still growing – and China gets lots of earthquakes.

The Himalayas are called **fold mountains**. Can you see why?

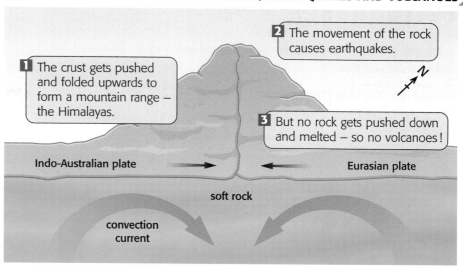

1 The crust gets pushed and folded upwards to form a mountain range – the Himalayas.

2 The movement of the rock causes earthquakes.

3 But no rock gets pushed down and melted – so no volcanoes!

Indo-Australian plate

Eurasian plate

soft rock

convection current

3 Some plates are sliding past each other

The Pacific plate is sliding past the North American plate. (Look at the map on page 111.)

Both move in the same direction, but the Pacific plate is moving faster.

The result is earthquakes now and then – but no volcanoes!

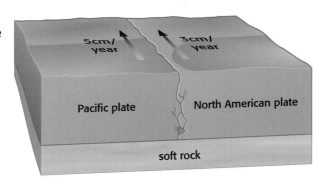

5cm/year   3cm/year

Pacific plate   North American plate

soft rock

1 Parts of the plates get stuck, then lurch free. This causes earthquakes.

2 But no rock gets pushed down and melted – so no volcanoes.

Your turn

1 The photo on the right shows the floor of the Atlantic Ocean. The grey ridge lies along plate edges.
   a Name the plates that lie on each side of the ridge.
   b What is the ridge made of?
   c Explain what is happening along the ridge.
   d Do you think earthquakes occur there? Explain.
   e Where else might you find a ridge like this?

2

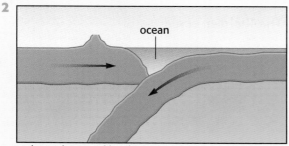

ocean

Make a drawing like this one. On your drawing:
   a label the ocean plate, the continental plate and a volcano.
   b mark in melted rock that feeds the volcano.
   c mark in and label an earthquake site.

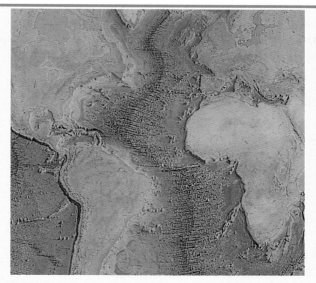

3 Now, using the maps on pages 111 and 128 – 129, explain why:
   a Peru has earthquakes and volcanoes
   b Iran has fold mountains
   c Italy has earthquakes and volcanoes
   d the UK has no active volcanoes.

Earthquakes

In this unit you'll learn what earthquakes are, and how they are measured, and what damage they do.

What is an earthquake?

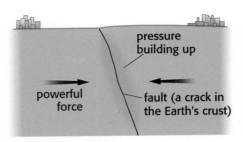

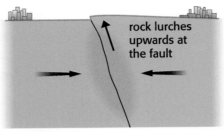

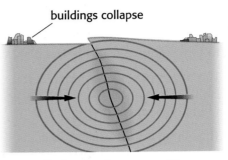

Imagine powerful forces pushing these huge masses of rock into each other. The rocks store up the pressure as **strain energy**.

But suddenly, the pressure gets too much. One mass of rock gives way, lurching upwards. The stored energy is released in waves …

… called **seismic waves**. These travel through the Earth in all directions, shaking everything. The shaking is called an **earthquake**.

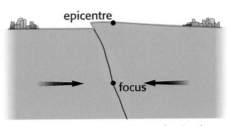

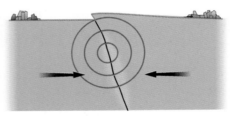

The **focus** of the earthquake is the point where the waves started. The **epicentre** is the point directly above it on the Earth's surface.

As the rock settles into its new position, there will be lots of smaller earthquakes called **aftershocks**.

Seismic waves get weaker as they travel. Even so, a large earthquake can still be detected thousands of kilometres away!

Any sudden large rock movement will cause an earthquake. That's why there are so many earthquakes along plate edges. But even the collapse of an old mine shaft, or an underground explosion, can cause a small earthquake.

How big?

- ◆ Earthquakes are measured using machines called **seismometers**, which record the shaking as waves on a graph.
- ◆ From the graph, scientists can tell how much energy the earthquake gave out.
- ◆ The amount of energy an earthquake gives out is called its **magnitude**.
- ◆ We show it on the **Richter scale**. (Look right.)
- ◆ An increase of 1 on this scale means the shaking is 10 times greater, and about 30 times more *energy* is given out. (And that means a lot more damage!)

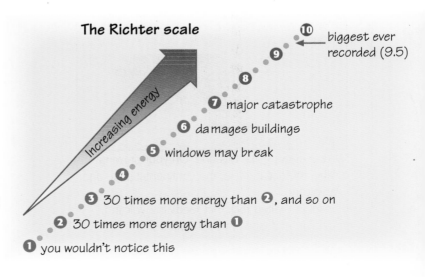

What damage can earthquakes do?

An earthquake shakes the ground, which then shakes everything on it. So …

Buildings and bridges crack and topple. Roads split open. Aftershocks make the damage worse.

Landslides may block roads.

Earthquakes in the ocean floor can cause giant waves called **tsunami** (say soonami) in shallow coastal water. They slam onto the land and do a huge amount of damage.

Water mains burst – which means no water.

Gas pipes fracture, and electricity wires get torn down. These cause fires.

Transport comes to a standstill.

At home, cookers and heaters fall over and start fires. Ceilings fall down. Doors jam. Everything slides off shelves and tables.

Your turn

1 Why do earthquakes happen so suddenly?

2 Explain in your own words what these earthquake terms mean. Use complete sentences.
   a seismic waves   b focus   c epicentre
   d magnitude   e seismometer

3 You are one of the people in the photo above. (Look carefully!) Describe what you see around you, in about 100 words.

4 Look at the earthquake diagram on the right.
   a Will the shaking be stronger at A, or at B? Explain.
   b Will the damage be greater at A, or at B? Why?
   c Will an earthquake of magnitude 7 do more damage than this one, or less? Why?
   d About how many times more energy will an earthquake of magnitude 7 give out, than this one?
   e An earthquake can occur at any time of day. When might an earthquake do more harm at B?
      i at 5 am   ii at 10.30 am
      Explain your answer.

5 The largest earthquake ever recorded was in 1960, *in the ocean off the coast of Chile*. It measured 9.5 on the Richter scale. Use the maps on pages 111 and 128–129 to help you answer these questions.
   a What do you think caused it?
   b It left 2 million people homeless in Chile. Explain how it managed to do that.
   c 22 hours later, it caused 200 people to drown on the east coast of Japan. How did it do that?

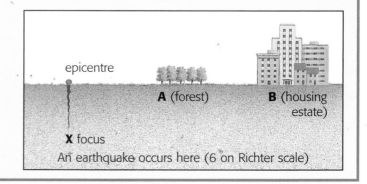

epicentre

A (forest)

B (housing estate)

X focus

An earthquake occurs here (6 on Richter scale)

Earthquake in Iran

In this unit you'll learn about an earthquake in Iran in 2003, and why it did so much damage.

The day Bam changed forever

The town of Bam in Iran is an oasis in the desert, where date palms and orange trees grow. In 2003, over 100 000 people lived in Bam. And many tourists came by to see its famous castle, over 2000 years old.

But on 26 December 2003, Bam changed forever. At 5.36 in the morning, while people were still asleep, an earthquake struck. It measured 6.5 on the Richter scale. It left 43 000 people dead and many thousands homeless. Over 70% of Bam lay in ruins, including the old castle.

Help floods in

News of the disaster shocked the world. The Iranian army and local people began the search for survivors. People came from all over Iran to help. Food, blankets, shelters, medicines, and money poured in from more than 20 other countries. Oxfam, the Red Cross, and other aid agencies sent people and equipment.

▲ One of a German rescue team, and his dog, search for survivors.

▲ A small corner of Bam, after the earthquake. Look how many buildings have collapsed.

◀ Not much left of the place they called home.

What caused the earthquake?

Like most earthquakes, this one was caused by plate movements.

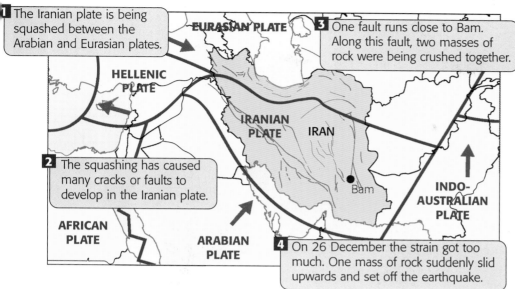

1 The Iranian plate is being squashed between the Arabian and Eurasian plates.

2 The squashing has caused many cracks or faults to develop in the Iranian plate.

3 One fault runs close to Bam. Along this fault, two masses of rock were being crushed together.

4 On 26 December the strain got too much. One mass of rock suddenly slid upwards and set off the earthquake.

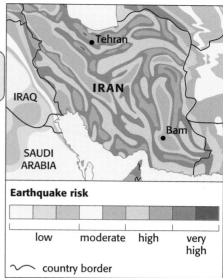

▲ *The earthquake risk across Iran.*

Earthquake risk

low   moderate   high   very high

country border

Why was there so much damage?

Sadly, much of Bam was built from mud bricks that cracked easily. And many people could not afford builders, so they built their own homes – badly. So, when the earthquake struck, most of the buildings collapsed, killing people asleep inside.

Grief – and anger

There was much grief in Iran about the deaths in Bam. There was also anger. 'We all know Iran is at risk from earthquakes' said one man, 'but we are not ready for them. We have building rules, but nobody pays much attention. The government does not enforce the rules. And they don't tell us what to do in earthquakes. They don't seem to have a plan.'

An earthquake to compare

At 4.31 am on 7 January 1994, an earthquake struck Northridge, a suburb of Los Angeles (California).

The earthquake measured 6.7 on the Richter scale. It left 57 people dead. 20% of the buildings were quite or very severely damaged, so many thousands were also left homeless.

Northridge has a population of around 60 000.

Your turn

1 Where is Iran? Say what continent it is on, and what countries border it. (Page 129 may help!)

2 Why did the earthquake happen? Explain in simple words, as if to a 7-year-old.

3 Look at the photo at the bottom of page 116. Imagine you are one of these two people. Write a diary entry describing what happened to your home and family on 26 December 2003, and how you feel about it.

4 Like Iran, the state of California in the USA is at high risk of earthquakes. Builders there are forced to make buildings earthquake-proof. The blue box above tells you about an earthquake in California.
  a Make a table like the one on the right.
  b Fill it in for the Bam and Northridge earthquakes.

c 'Stronger buildings in Bam would have saved many lives.' Do you agree? Give evidence from your table.

5 Look at the earthquake risk map for Iran, above.
  a Is Bam likely to have more earthquakes?
  b The president of Iran promised that Bam will be rebuilt. You are an engineer. Write a letter to the president with advice about rebuilding the town.

Comparing two earthquakes

Location	Bam, Iran	Northridge, USA
Magnitude		
% of population killed		
% of buildings damaged/ destroyed		
Are strict rules in force for seismic-proof buildings?		

Volcanoes

In this unit you'll learn what volcanoes are, and what damage an eruption can do.

What's a volcano?

A **volcano** is where liquid rock or **magma** shoots out or **erupts** through the ground. Above ground, the liquid rock is called **lava**.

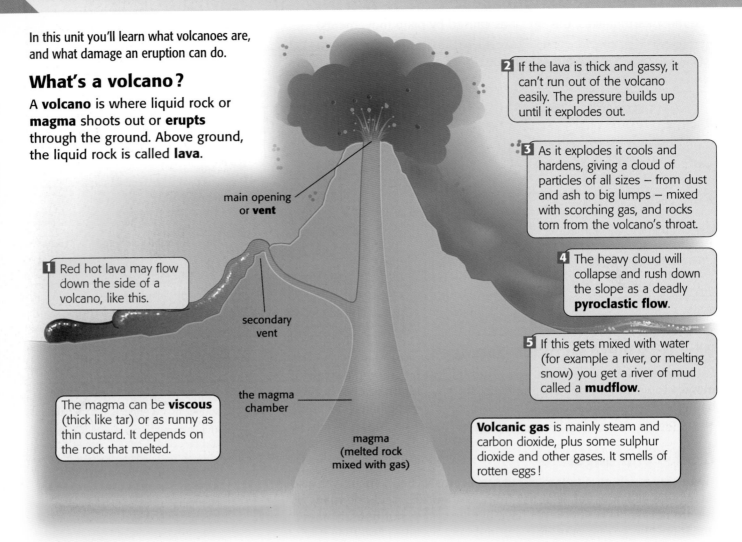

main opening or **vent**

secondary vent

the magma chamber

magma (melted rock mixed with gas)

1 Red hot lava may flow down the side of a volcano, like this.

The magma can be **viscous** (thick like tar) or as runny as thin custard. It depends on the rock that melted.

2 If the lava is thick and gassy, it can't run out of the volcano easily. The pressure builds up until it explodes out.

3 As it explodes it cools and hardens, giving a cloud of particles of all sizes – from dust and ash to big lumps – mixed with scorching gas, and rocks torn from the volcano's throat.

4 The heavy cloud will collapse and rush down the slope as a deadly **pyroclastic flow**.

5 If this gets mixed with water (for example a river, or melting snow) you get a river of mud called a **mudflow**.

Volcanic gas is mainly steam and carbon dioxide, plus some sulphur dioxide and other gases. It smells of rotten eggs!

Viscous gassy lava is the most dangerous kind. It builds up inside the volcano. Then the gas propels it out in an explosion.

▲ An eruption of runny lava in Hawaii.

▲ A small eruption of steam, gas and ash from Mt St Helens (USA). The hollow around the vent is called a **crater**.

What damage can eruptions do?

The dust from an explosive eruption may rise high in the atmosphere and block out the sun, causing temperatures around the world to fall.

A pyroclastic flow travels at up to 200 km an hour. You can't escape. It scorches and smothers everything.

Volcanic gas causes acid rain. This kills trees and plants over a wide area.

The dust can also cause planes to crash.

Mudflows can travel at 100 km an hour. They sweep everything along. You drown in mud.

A thick blanket of ash will ruin crops.

Lava flows destroy crops, and bury towns and villages. (They could kill you too – but you can just walk out of the way.)

A thick layer of ash is heavy enough to make roofs collapse.

The ash from an explosive eruption gets everywhere – in your eyes, your hair, your lungs. It can suffocate you.

The photo above was taken on Montserrat. Find out more on the next page!

Your turn

1 What is: **a** magma? **b** lava?

2 Make a larger copy of this drawing.
  Then colour it in and add the missing labels.

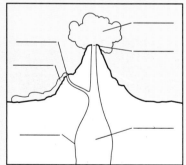

3 Look at the photo above.
  What do you think happened to:
  a the roof of the church? **b** the trees near the church?

4 An active volcano can give out all of these:
  showers of ash   a pyrocolastic flow   a lava flow
  plumes of dust   volcanic gases
  a List them in order of danger, starting with what you think is the most dangerous one.
  b Beside each item in your list, say what harm it does.

5 You were there when Mount Pinatubo in the Philippines erupted, in 1991. You took the photo below. E-mail your friend in New York telling him what you saw before you took it – and what happened next.

119

Montserrat: a volcano awakens

In this unit you will learn how an erupting volcano has changed a Caribbean island forever.

A paradise island

At the start of 1995, 11 000 people lived on the island of Montserrat in the Caribbean. Some farmed for a living. Some worked in the island's few factories. But most depended on the tourists who came to enjoy the peace on this paradise isle.

Then, on 18 July, life on the island began to change forever. The volcano, asleep for nearly 400 years, began to waken.

The volcano awakens

The first signs were rumbling noises, and showers of ash, and a strong smell of sulphur. The government acted quickly. It called in **vulcanologists** (volcano scientists) to check or **monitor** the volcano, and made plans to move people to safety.

That was way back in 1995. The volcano has been busy ever since!

- ◆ It has blasted out clouds of dust and ash that turned the sky black.
- ◆ It has grown domes full of lava that glowed at night before exploding.
- ◆ It has given pyroclastic flows that raced down the slopes. Some turned rivers into mudflows.

The vulcanologists watch it night and day. But they can't predict when it will go back to sleep again.

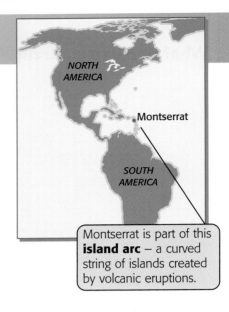

Montserrat is part of this **island arc** – a curved string of islands created by volcanic eruptions.

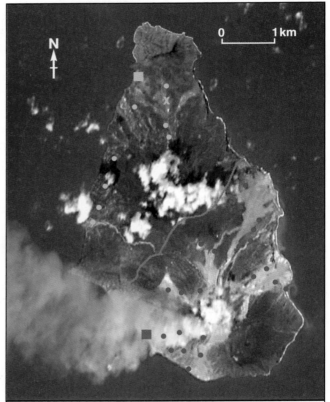

▼ *Montserrat from the air. Spot the volcano !*

Key

■	capital (Plymouth) destroyed
X	airport (destroyed)
●	small settlements, abandoned or destroyed
∿	out-of-bounds below this line
▪	proposed new capital (Little Bay)
X	new airport (2005)
●	undamaged small settlements

◀ *Just another pyroclastic flow on Montserrat.*

What's causing the eruptions?

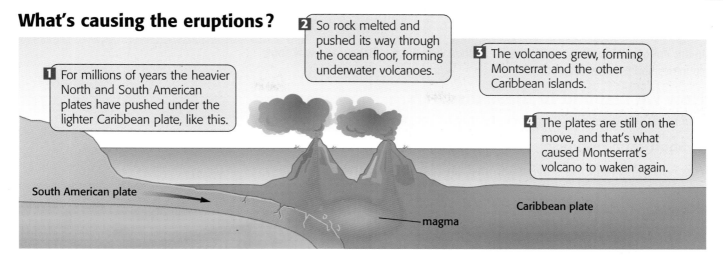

1 For millions of years the heavier North and South American plates have pushed under the lighter Caribbean plate, like this.

2 So rock melted and pushed its way through the ocean floor, forming underwater volcanoes.

3 The volcanoes grew, forming Montserrat and the other Caribbean islands.

4 The plates are still on the move, and that's what caused Montserrat's volcano to waken again.

South American plate

Caribbean plate

magma

People on the move

As the volcano grew more dangerous, people were moved from the south of the island. Some went to the 'safe' area in the north, to stay with friends or in shelters. Some went to other Caribbean islands, or to relatives abroad. By April 1996 the south of the island was empty.

But some refused to stay away. On 25 June 1997, pyroclastic flows killed 19 people who had crept back to work on their farms.

Life goes on

Today, only 4500 people are left on Montserrat, in the north of the island. The south is still out of bounds. (If you are caught there you will be fined and may even be sent to prison.)

There is not much farming now, since so much of the land is ruined. And there are very few tourists. The people depend on grants from the UK and the European Union. Now their main work is building – houses for the refugees, schools, roads and a new airport.

But they can't forget about the volcano. Every so often a dark plume in the sky, or a shower of ash, or a rattle of pebbles, reminds them.

▲ *Out of action… forever?*

Your turn

1 Explain in your own words why the volcano on Montserrat is erupting.

2 Look at the photo on page 106. It shows Plymouth, the capital of Montserrat, destroyed by the volcano. You used to live there. Write a letter to your cousin in Burnley describing what Plymouth looks like now.

3 How will the eruptions on Montserrat have affected:
   a farmers?   b hotel owners?   c taxi drivers?

4 Montserrat hopes to attact tourists again – as a volcano island! You are in charge of tourism.
   a Draw a sketch map of the island, showing the volcano, the new airport, and the safe zone.
   b Mark in where you would put a new tourist hotel.
   c What activities will you lay on for tourists?
   d How will you make sure the tourists are safe?
   e What kind of souvenirs will you sell them?
   f Make up a slogan to attract tourists to the island.

5 Montserrat has received nearly £200 million in aid, since the volcano awoke. Most was from the UK, since it's a British colony. Some people think that the island should just be closed down.
   a Give some arguments in favour of this.
   b Give some arguments against it.
   c If you had to make the final decision, what other information would you need?

Coping with earthquakes and eruptions

In this unit you'll learn how we cope with earthquakes and eruptions – and why some countries find it harder than others.

How we respond to these disasters

When earthquakes and eruptions destroy places, we respond in two ways.

1 Short-term response

First, we try to help the survivors in the days and weeks ahead.

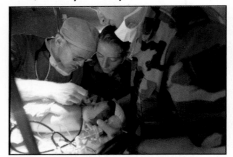

Doctors, nurses, firemen and the army rush there. Medical tents are set up. Aid agencies like Oxfam and the Red Cross arrive.

Tents, food, water and clothing are given to the people who have lost their homes. (These may be gifts from other countries.)

Ordinary people like you and me give money to help the survivors of the disaster rebuild their lives and homes.

2 Long-term response

Then we try to prevent disasters like this happening in the future.

We can't stop earthquakes and eruptions. But at least we can identify the areas at risk.

Then we can make plans to protect the people living in these areas. Some of the plans …

… can be put into action right away – for example plans to make buildings more quake-proof.

Other plans will be put into action the next time there's an emergency.

Meanwhile, scientists can monitor the areas at risk, and try to predict when earthquakes or eruptions …

… will happen, so that they can warn people in time to move to a safe place.

Your turn

1 **A–G** below match words or terms used on page 122. For each, you have to pick out the matching word or term. Set out your answers like this:

B for the months and years ahead = long–t…

A for the next days and weeks
B for the months and years ahead
C a sudden dangerous situation
D to observe and check and take measurements
E to tell in advance when something will happen
F they study rocks (and earthquakes!)
G they collect money to help people in need
The glossary might help!

2 There is a big **earthquake** in a city in South America. 80 000 people are killed.
A–J below are responses to the disaster.

a Make a big table with headings like this:

Responses to the earthquake disaster	
Short-term	Long-term

b Now write out the sentences **A–J** in the correct columns. (With their label letters!)

A 30 firemen fly in from Italy to help.
B The government sets up a team of geologists to try to predict future earthquakes.
C A law is passed that all new buildings must be built to cope with shaking.
D All bridges in the city are made stronger.
E South American countries set up a joint satellite system, to monitor plate movements.
F From now on, all schools in the country will teach pupils what to do in an earthquake.
G A city hospital sets up a tent for the injured.
H Reporters arrive from all over the world.
I Spain gives $500 million to help rebuild the city.
J In Leeds, Form 3A collects £80 for the survivors.

3 Which of the responses above are:
a local (in the hit city)? b national?
c international?
To answer, underline each type of response in a different colour, in your table.
Then add a colour key.

4 Now, imagine there's a huge **volcanic eruption** in Mexico that kills 9000 people. Make up six examples of responses to the disaster. You must include:
- at least two international responses
- at least one involving an aid agency
- at least one involving scientists.

5

This photo shows a sad father in Bam, after the earthquake in 2003. His children were buried by the earthquake. They were dug out after two days – but they died later in a tent hospital.
The things below might have helped to keep them safe. For each, try to explain why.
a a team of inspectors to enforce strict building rules
b money to buy strong building materials
c lots of money for research into predicting earthquakes, in that country
d a good motorway network
e better emergency plans for earthquakes
f well equipped hospitals

6 The trouble is – protecting people from disasters costs a lot of money! Look at the table below. It gives data for three countries at risk of earthquakes.
a Which of the three is wealthiest? (Glossary?)
b Which do you think is most likely to be able to:
   i help people injured in disasters?
   ii protect people from disasters in the long-term?
   Give reasons for your answers.

Comparing some countries			
Country	Iran	Mexico	USA
GDP per capita	$6000	$8430	$34 320
Number of TVs per 1000 people	172	282	937
Number of doctors per 10 000 people	11	14	28
Number of hospital beds per 10 000 people	16	11	36
Length of motorway per 1000 sq km of the country	0.54 km	3.34 km	8.17 km

Why live in a danger zone?

In this unit you'll find out why people still live near plate edges, even though it's dangerous. And also about ways that plate movements benefit us!

Crazy or what?

Millions of people live near plate edges, where there's a high risk of earthquakes and eruptions. Why don't they move somewhere safer?

Did you know?
- About 1 in 12 of us lives in a danger zone (near a plate edge).
- That's about 500 million people!

People settled in danger zones before we understood the risks. (We didn't know about plates until the 1960's.)

Some of the settlements have now grown into enormous cities – like Mexico and Tokyo. Where could all those people move to?

Lots of us think disasters happen only to other people. We ignore the dangers and get on with our lives.

Many are too poor to move. And even after a disaster, some want to return to the life they know best.

A good job and a good way of life may keep you in a danger zone, even if you feel a little nervous.

Places like California and Japan are well prepared for earthquakes. This makes people feel safe.

▲ One of the world's most visited volcanoes – Mount Fuji, Japan.

▲ Lava threatens a vineyard on Mount Etna, Italy.

Now for the good news!

You've met the bad news – plate movements can kill. The good news is: they also bring benefits – thanks mainly to volcanoes.

Good soil. Lava breaks down to give very fertile soil. On Mount Etna in Sicily, farmers grow rich crops of grapes and other fruit. In Java and Japan they grow rice.

Money from tourism. Volcanic areas attract tourists, and tourists spend money! They flock to visit Mount Etna and Mount Fuji, and the volcanoes of Iceland. They can see **geysers** and **fumaroles**, and relax in hot springs.

Geothermal energy or energy from hot rock. In some volcanic areas, water is pumped down onto the hot rocks. It comes back up as steam. This is used to heat homes, or to drive turbines for making electricity.

Over 70% of the homes in Iceland use geothermal energy.

Valuable materials. Copper, silver, gold and lead are found in extinct volcanoes. (They collect in veins when magma hardens again.) Sulphur is mined around old volcano vents. Basalt is used to build roads.

Fossil fuels. Plate movements cause lush vegetation to get buried. Over millions of years it turns into **coal**. They also cause dead sea creatures to get buried – and these turn into **oil** and **gas**. We depend on these fuels.

As the population of the Earth grows, even more people will live in danger zones. We need to get better at predicting earthquakes and eruptions, and protecting people from harm.

▲ Don't get too close to a geyser! This one is in Yellowstone National Park, Wyoming, USA.

Your turn

1 Using the world map on pages 128–129, and the plate map on page 111, name six capital cities that appear to be in danger zones.

2 Give:
   a two economic reasons   b two social reasons
   why people continue to live in danger zones.

3 Do you agree with this person? Give reasons.

4 Give all the ways plate movements help *you*. (For example, gas for cooking.) You could draw a spider map to answer.

MOVE EVERYONE OUT OF DANGER ZONES NOW!

5 Can you think of anyone who benefits from earthquakes? Give as many examples as you can.

6 What is: a a geyser?   b a fumarole? (Try the glossary.)

7 You are an engineer. Copy this drawing and complete it to show how you could heat these homes.

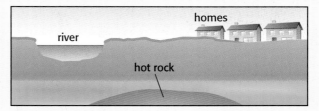

homes
river
hot rock

Ordnance Survey symbols

ROADS AND PATHS

M I or A 6(M)	Motorway
A 35	Dual carriageway
A 31(T) or A 35	Trunk or main road
B 3074	Secondary road
	Narrow road with passing places
	Road under construction
	Road generally more than 4 m wide
	Road generally less than 4 m wide
	Other road, drive or track, fenced and unfenced
	Gradient: steeper than 1 in 5; 1 in 7 to 1 in 5
Ferry	Ferry; Ferry P – passenger only
	Path

PUBLIC RIGHTS OF WAY

(Not applicable to Scotland)

1:25 000	1:50 000	
		Footpath
		Road used as a public footpath
+++++++		Bridleway
		Byway open to all traffic

RAILWAYS

	Multiple track
	Single track
	Narrow gauge/Light rapid transit system
	Road over; road under; level crossing
	Cutting; tunnel; embankment
	Station, open to passengers; siding

BOUNDARIES

+ — + — +	National
+ — + — +	District
— · — · — · —	County, Unitary Authority, Metropolitan District or London Borough
	National Park

HEIGHTS/ROCK FEATURES

———50———	Contour lines
· 144	Spot height to the nearest metre above sea level

outcrop cliff scree

ABBREVIATIONS

P	Post office	PC	Public convenience (rural areas)
PH	Public house	TH	Town Hall, Guildhall or equivalent
MS	Milestone	Sch	School
MP	Milepost	Coll	College
CH	Clubhouse	Mus	Museum
CG	Coastguard	Cemy	Cemetery
Fm	Farm		

ANTIQUITIES

VILLA	Roman	⚔	Battlefield (with date)
Castle	Non-Roman	✶	Tumulus

LAND FEATURES

	Buildings
	Public building
	Bus or coach station
	Place of Worship { with tower / with spire, minaret or dome / without such additions }
∘	Chimney or tower
	Glass structure
Ⓗ	Heliport
△	Triangulation pillar
	Mast
	Wind pump / wind generator
	Windmill
+	Graticule intersection
	Cutting, embankment
	Quarry
	Spoil heap, refuse tip or dump
	Coniferous wood
	Non-coniferous wood
	Mixed wood
	Orchard
	Park or ornamental ground
	Forestry Commission access land
	National Trust – always open
	National Trust, limited access, observe local signs
	National Trust for Scotland

TOURIST INFORMATION

P	Parking
V	Visitor centre
i	Information centre
✆	Telephone
	Camp site/Caravan site
	Golf course or links
	Viewpoint
PC	Public convenience
	Picnic site
	Pub/s
	Cathedral/Abbey
	Museum
	Castle/fort
	Building of historic interest
	English Heritage
	Garden
	Nature reserve
	Water activities
	Fishing
☆	Other tourist feature

WATER FEATURES

Marsh or salting, Towpath, Lock, Slopes, Cliff, Flat rock, High water mark, Low water mark, Aqueduct, Canal, Ford, Normal tidal limit, Sand, Dunes, Lighthouse (in use), Beacon, Lake, Weir, Bridge, Footbridge, Mud, Lighthouse (disused), Shingle, Canal (dry)

Map of the British Isles

Key

- ------ international boundary
- —— national boundary
- ～ river
- lake
- ▲ highest point in the UK

towns

- ■ largest cities
- ● large cities and towns

Land height

measured in metres above sea level

- more than 1000 m
- 500 - 1000 m
- 200 - 500 m
- 100 - 200 m
- less than 100 m
- land below sea level

Scale

1: 4 500 000

One centimetre on the map represents 45 kilometres on the ground.

0   45   90   135   180 km

Transverse Mercator Projection

Shetland Islands

Orkney Islands

Cape Wrath

Outer Hebrides

Lewis

Skye

NORTHWEST HIGHLANDS

Great Glen

Loch Ness

River Spey

CAIRNGORMS

River Dee

Aberdeen

1344m ▲ Ben Nevis

GRAMPIAN MOUNTAINS

R. Tay

Mull

SCOTLAND

Dundee

Loch Lomond

Islay

Glasgow

River Clyde

Edinburgh

Firth of Forth

Firth of Clyde

SOUTHERN UPLANDS

R. Tweed

UNITED KINGDOM

CHEVIOT HILLS

Warkworth

R. Coquet

NORTH ATLANTIC OCEAN

NORTHERN IRELAND

R. Bann

ANTRIM MOUNTAINS

Lough Neagh

River Erne

Belfast

North Channel

Isle of Man

Newcastle upon Tyne

River Tyne

Sunderland

Stockton-on-Tees

Middlesbrough

Darlington

NORTH YORK MOORS

North Sea

River Eden

LAKE DISTRICT

River Tees

PENNINES

REPUBLIC OF IRELAND

Lough Corrib

R. Boyne

River Shannon

R. Liffey

Dublin

WICKLOW MOUNTAINS

Irish Sea

Blackpool

Preston

Bradford

Leeds

River Ouse

Kingston-upon-Hull

Huddersfield

River Aire

Bolton

Manchester

Liverpool

Stockport

Warrington

River Mersey

Sheffield

River Humber

Anglesey

R. Dee

ENGLAND

R. Trent

The Wash

Stoke-on-Trent

Lough Corrib

Barrow

River Suir

River Blackwater

Cork

River Liffey

River Shannon

Cardigan Bay

CAMBRIAN MOUNTAINS

Shrewsbury

Derby

Nottingham

Telford

Leicester

THE FENS

R. Wensum

Norwich

Walsall

Wolverhampton

Birmingham

Coventry

Peterborough

Dudley

Solihull

Northampton

R. Great Ouse

Ipswich

R. Stour

WALES

River Teifi

BRECON BEACONS

River Tywi

River Usk

R. Wye

R. Severn

River Avon

COTSWOLD HILLS

Milton Keynes

Luton

Aylesbury

CHILTERN HILLS

Basildon

Southend-on-Sea

Swansea

Newport

Cardiff

R. Thames

Reading

London

Arsenal FC (grounds)

Greenwich

NORTH DOWNS

St George's Channel

NORTH ATLANTIC OCEAN

Bristol Channel

Bristol

SALISBURY PLAIN

SOUTH DOWNS

Strait of Dover

EXMOOR

R. Exe

Southampton

Bournemouth

Poole

Portsmouth

Brighton

DARTMOOR

Isle of Wight

Torbay

Plymouth

Land's End

Isles of Scilly

English Channel

127

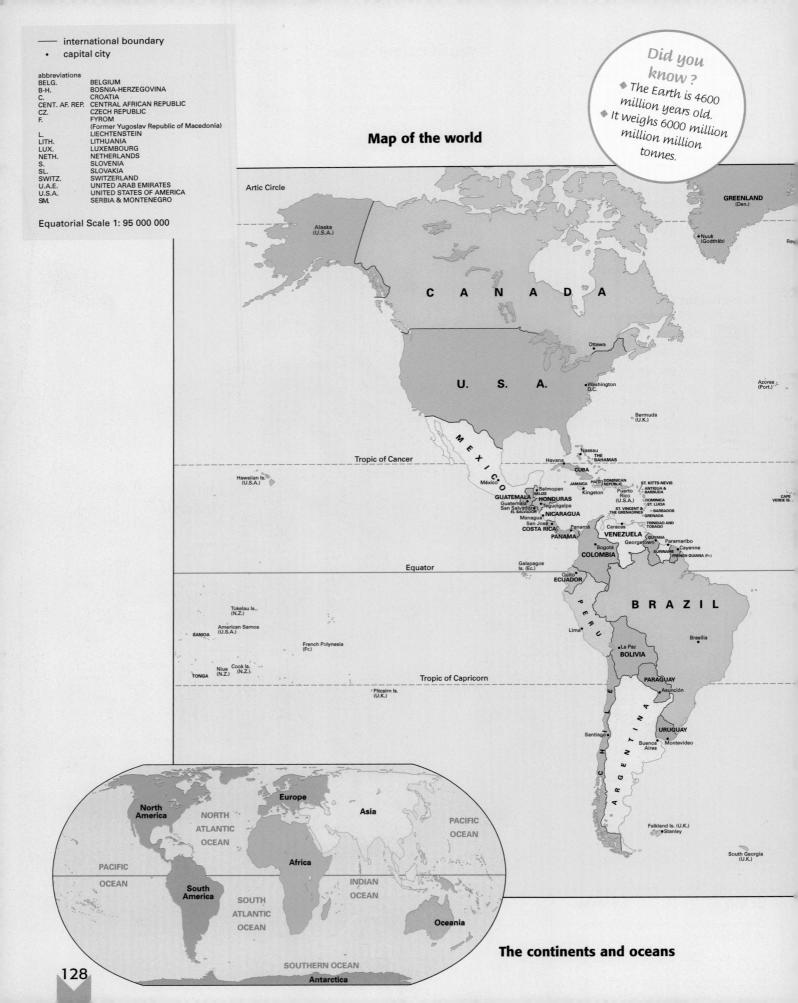

Map of the world

Did you know ?
◆ The Earth is 4600 million years old.
◆ It weighs 6000 million million million tonnes.

Artic Circle

GREENLAND (Den.)

Alaska (U.S.A.)

Nuuk (Godthåb)

Rey

C A N A D A

Ottawa

U. S. A.

Washington D.C.

Azores (Port.)

Bermuda (U.K.)

M E X I C O

Tropic of Cancer

México

Havana

Nassau
THE BAHAMAS

CUBA

Hawaiian Is. (U.S.A.)

Belmopan
BELIZE

GUATEMALA

JAMAICA

HAITI

DOMINICAN REPUBLIC

ST. KITTS-NEVIS
ANTIGUA & BARBUDA

Guatemala
San Salvador
EL SALVADOR

HONDURAS

Tegucigalpa

Kingston

Puerto Rico (U.S.A.)

DOMINICA
ST. LUCIA

CAPE VERDE IS.

Managua

NICARAGUA

ST. VINCENT & THE GRENADINES

BARBADOS
GRENADA

San José
COSTA RICA

Panamá

Caracas

TRINIDAD AND TOBAGO

PANAMA

VENEZUELA

Georgetown

Paramaribo

Cayenne

Bogotá

GUYANA

SURINAME

FRENCH GUIANA (Fr.)

COLOMBIA

Galapagos Is. (Ec.)

Equator

Quito
ECUADOR

B R A Z I L

Tokelau Is. (N.Z.)

P
E
R
U

Lima

Brasília

American Samoa (U.S.A.)

SAMOA

French Polynesia (Fr.)

La Paz
BOLIVIA

TONGA

Niue (N.Z.)

Cook Is. (N.Z.)

Tropic of Capricorn

PARAGUAY

Asunción

Pitcairn Is. (U.K.)

C
H
I
L
E

A
R
G
E
N
T
I
N
A

URUGUAY

Santiago

Buenos Aires

Montevideo

Falkland Is. (U.K.)
Stanley

South Georgia (U.K.)

North America

Europe

Asia

NORTH ATLANTIC OCEAN

PACIFIC OCEAN

PACIFIC OCEAN

Africa

South America

INDIAN OCEAN

SOUTH ATLANTIC OCEAN

Oceania

SOUTHERN OCEAN

Antarctica

The continents and oceans

Amazing – but true!
- ◆ Nearly 70% of the Earth is covered by saltwater.
- ◆ Nearly 1/3 is covered by the Pacific Ocean.
- ◆ 10% of the land is covered by glaciers.
- ◆ 20% of the land is covered by deserts.

World champions
- ◆ Largest continent – Asia
- ◆ Longest river – The Nile, Egypt
- ◆ Highest mountain – Everest, Nepal
- ◆ Largest desert – Sahara, North Africa
- ◆ Largest ocean – Pacific

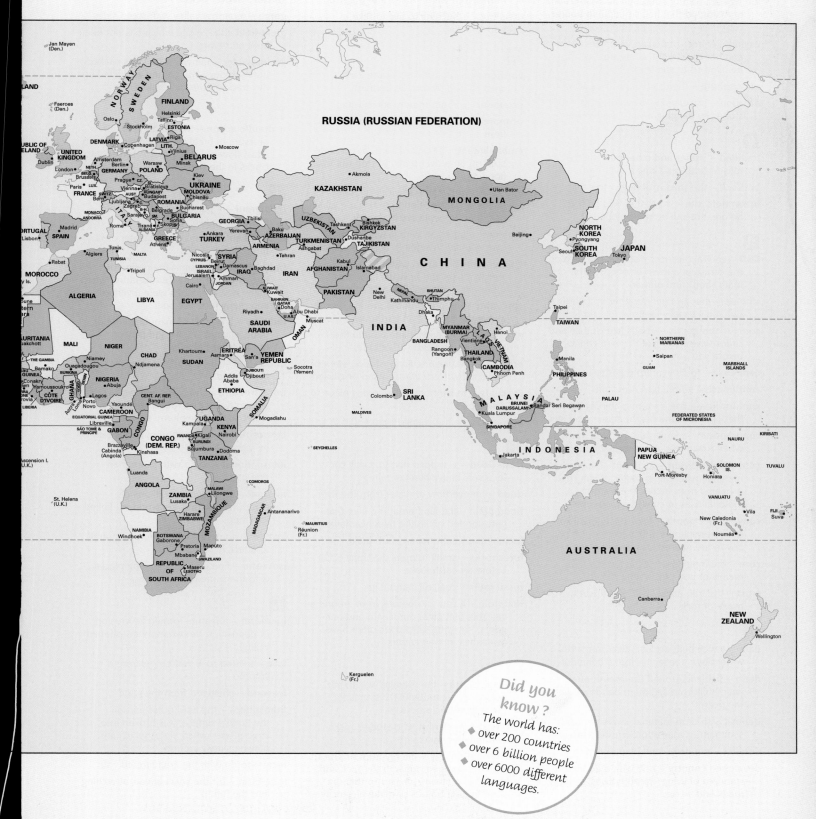

Did you know?
The world has:
- ◆ over 200 countries
- ◆ over 6 billion people
- ◆ over 6000 different languages.

Glossary

A

abrasion – the scraping of a river bed and banks by stones and sand in the river

aid agency – an organisation such as Oxfam or ActionAid that helps people in poorer countries (including in emergencies)

asylum seeker – a person who flees to another country for safety, and asks to be allowed to stay there

atmosphere – the gas around the Earth

attrition – the wearing down of rocks and stones by banging against each other

B

bedload – stones and other material that rolls or bounces along a river bed

bedrock – the solid rock below the soil

brownfield site – a site that was built on before, but can be redeveloped

C

CBD – central business district – the area at the centre of a town or city with the main shops and offices

climate – the 'average' weather in a place (what it's usually like)

comparison goods – goods like clothes and shoes where you like to see a choice before you buy

condense – to change from gas to liquid

confluence – where two rivers join

contour line – line on a map joining places that are the same height above sea level

conurbation – a large built-up area formed when towns and cities spread and join

convection current – a current of warmer material; when air or water or soft rock is heated from below, the warmer material rises in convection currents

convenience goods – low-cost goods like milk, newspapers and sweets which you buy in the nearest convenient place

core – the inner layer of the Earth, made mainly of iron plus a little nickel

crust – the thin outer layer of the Earth, made of rock

D

dam – a wall built across a river to control water flow; a reservoir forms behind it

delta – flat land around the mouth of a river, built from sediment deposited by the river

deposit – to drop material; rivers deposit sediment as they approach the sea

derelict – run-down and abandoned

developed country – one with a good standard of living - good houses, schools, roads and so on

developers – companies that buy land and put up buildings for rent or sale

drainage basin – the land around a river, from which water drains into the river

dwelling – a building to live in (like a house or flat)

E

earthquake – the shaking of the Earth's crust caused by rock movement

economic – about money and business

economic activity – work you earn money from

embankment – a bank of earth or concrete built up on a river bank, to stop the river flooding

emergency services – services such as police, ambulance and fire brigade which help when people are in danger

emigrant – a person who leaves his or her own country to settle in another country

environmental – to do with our surroundings and how we look after them (air, rivers, wildlife and so on)

epicentre – the point on the ground directly above the focus of an earthquake

equator – an imaginary line around the middle of the Earth (0° latitude)

erosion – the wearing away of rock, stones and soil by rivers, waves, wind or glaciers

evacuate – move from a dangerous place to a safe one

evaporation – the change from liquid to gas

F

flash flood – a sudden flood usually caused by a very heavy burst of rain

flood – an overflow of water from the river

flood plain – flat land around a river that gets flooded when the river overflows

focus – the 'centre' of an earthquake

foreshocks – small tremors that may occur before an earthquake

fossil fuels – coal, oil, natural gas

fumarole – a vent or opening in or around a volcano, that gives out steam and hot gases; 'sleeping' volcanoes often have fumaroles in their craters

G

GDP per capita – the average wealth per person, in a country (GDP stands for gross domestic product)

geologist – a scientist who studies rocks, earthquakes and so on

geothermal energy – energy from hot rock; water is pumped down to the rock and turned into steam, which can then be used to heat homes or make electricity

geyser – a burst of boiling water and steam from the ground; it is groundwater that has been boiled up by hot rock

glacier – a river of ice

gorge – a narrow valley with steep sides

greenfield site – a site which has not been built on before

groundwater – rainwater that has soaked down through the ground and filled up the cracks in the rock below

H

hydraulic action – the action of water pressure in breaking up a river bank; in a fast flowing river, water is forced into cracks in the bank, making them larger

I

immigrant – a person who comes into a country to live

impermeable – does not let water pass through

Industrial Revolution – the period of history (around the 18th century) when many new machines were invented and many factories built

industry – a branch of manufacturing or trade, such as the car industry or the building industry

infiltration – the soaking of rainwater into the ground

infrastructure – the basic services in a country, such as roads, railways, water supply, telephone system

interception – the capture of rainwater by leaves

international – to do with more than one country

internet – a network of millions of computers around the world, all linked together

invader – someone who enters a country to attack it

isotherm – line on a map joining places with the same temperature

L

landform – a feature formed by erosion or deposition (for example a V-shaped valley)

lava – melted rock that erupts from a volcano

leeward – sheltered from the wind

lithosphere – the hard outer part of the Earth's surface; it is broken into large pieces called plates which are moving slowly around

local – to do with the area around you

long-term – for the years ahead, stretching into the future

M

magma – melted rock below the Earth's surface; when it reaches the surface it is called lava

magnitude – how much energy an earthquake gives out

mantle – the middle layer of the Earth, between the crust and the core

meander – a bend in a river

media – forms of communication, such as TV, radio, newspapers, the internet

merchandise – goods for sale

migrant – a person who moves to another part of the country or another country, often just to work for a while

monsoon – the season in south-east Asia when warm moist winds blow in from the sea, bringing lots of rain

mudflow – a river of mud; it can form when the material from an eruption mixes with rain or melting ice

N

national – to do with the whole country (for example the national anthem)

North Atlantic Drift – a warm current in the Atlantic Ocean; it keeps the weather on the west coast of Britain mild in winter

O

oxbow lake – a lake formed when a loop in a river gets cut off

P

peninsula – a piece of land almost surrounded by water

permeable – lets water soak through

persecute – to punish or treat cruelly (for example because of race or religion)

plan – a map of a small area (such as the school, or a room) drawn to scale

plates – the Earth's surface is broken into large pieces, like a cracked eggshell; the pieces are called plates

plunge pool – deep pool below a waterfall

population density – the average number of people per square kilometre

pothole – holes down through rock, caused by weathering and erosion

precipitation – water falling from the sky (as rain, sleet, hail, snow)

prevailing winds – the ones that blow most often; in the UK they are south west winds (blowing *from* the south west)

primary sector – the part of the economy where people take things from the Earth and sea (farming, fishing, mining)

pyroclastic flow – a flood of gas, dust, ash and other particles rushing down the side of a volcano, after an eruption

Q

quaternary sector – the part of the economy where people do high-tech research (for example into genes)

R

rain shadow – area sheltered from the rain by a hill or mountain

redevelop – to rebuild an area for a new use

refugee – a person who has been forced to flee from danger (for example from war)

residential area – an area which is mainly homes (rather than shops or offices)

Richter scale – a scale for measuring the energy given out in an earthquake

Ring of Fire – the ring of volcanoes around the Pacific Ocean

rural area – countryside, where people live on farms and in small villages

S

saltation – the bouncing movement of sand and small stones along a river bed

scale – the ratio of the distance on a map to the real distance

secondary sector – the part of the economy where people make or manufacture things (such as cars or furniture)

sediment – a layer of material (stones, sand and mud) deposited by a river

seismic wave – wave of energy given out in an earthquake; it shakes everything

seismometer – an instrument for recording the vibrations during an earthquake

service – something set up to meet people's needs; for example a shop, a school, a library, a hospital

settlement – a place where people live; it could be a hamlet, village, town or city

settlement hierarchy – settlements in order of size, with the largest one first

settler – a person who takes over land to live on, where no one has lived before

short-term – just for the days and weeks (and perhaps months) ahead

silt – fine particles of soil carried by rivers

site – the land a settlement is built on

situation – the position of a settlement in relation to features such as rivers, hills and other settlements

sketch map – a simple map to show what a place is like, or how to get there; it is not drawn to scale

social – about society and our way of life

soil – a mixture of clay, sand and the remains of dead plants; it forms when rock is broken down by weathering

solution – the dissolving of minerals from a river bed and banks, by the water

source – the starting point of a river

sphere of influence – area around a settlement (or shop, or other service) where its influence is felt

spot height – the exact height at a spot on an OS map (look for a dot and number)

suspension – small particles of rock and soil carried along in a river; they make the water look cloudy or muddy

sustainable – will not harm people, wildlife, or the environment, into the future

T

tertiary sector – the part of the economy where people provide services (for example teachers, doctors, taxi drivers)

throughflow – the flow of rainwater sideways through the soil

traction – the rolling movement of rocks and stones along a river bed

trench – deep V-shaped valley in the ocean floor

tributary – a river that flows into a larger one

U

urban area – a built-up area, such as a town or city

urban regeneration – when a run-down urban area is redeveloped and brought to life again

U-shaped valley – a valley shaped like the letter U, carved out by a glacier

V

vale – a very broad open valley

valley – an area of low land, with higher land on each side; it often has a river flowing in it

vent – a hole through which lava erupts, on a volcano

volcano – a place where lava erupts at the Earth's surface

vulcanologist – a scientist who studies volcanoes

V-shaped valley – a valley shaped like the letter V, carved out by a river

W

water cycle – the non-stop cycle in which water evaporates from the sea, falls as rain, and returns to the sea in rivers

water vapour – water in gas form

waterfall – where a river or stream flows over a steep drop

watershed – an imaginary line separating one drainage basin from the next

weather – the state of the atmosphere – for example how warm or wet or windy it is

weathering – the breaking down of rock

windward – facing into the wind

Index